Jim Selley

PREHISTORIC AMERICA

Second Edition

PREHISTORIC

AN ECOLOGICAL PERSPECTIVE

ALDINE PUBLISHING COMPANY/NEW YORK

Betty J. Meggers

SMITHSONIAN INSTITUTION

AMERICA

Second edition published by
Aldine Publishing Company
200 Saw Mill River Road
Hawthorne, New York 10532

ISBN 0-202-3307-8 cloth; 0-202-33079-6 paper

Printed in the United States of America
Designed by John Goetz

Preface
to the Second Edition

Since the first edition of this book appeared in 1972, thousands of additional sites have been recorded and hundreds of thousands of artifacts have been studied. Palynologists, sedimentologists, botanists, and zoologists have provided reconstructions of climate, vegetation, and diet. Hundreds of carbon-14 dates have been obtained. Sophisticated chemical and physical methods have been employed to identify the sources of rocks and minerals found in occupation refuse, to thereby reconstruct systems of exchange. Experiments have improved our understanding of the manufacture and use of stone tools. Experts on basketry and lithic technology can even recognize idiosyncracies that reveal the number of artisans in the extinct community. Although many parts of the hemisphere remain poorly known, the data base is several times greater than it was only seven years ago.

When we examine the impact of this new knowledge on the major issues of New World prehistory, however, we find it surprisingly small. Disagreement persists over whether human beings reached North America before the end of the last glaciation, although more authorities now accept a minimal antiquity of ± 30,000 years. The existence of a "Pre-Projectile Point" stage is unresolved. The ancestry of maize remains disputed. Whether transpacific contacts occurred and, if so, whether they had significant effects on New World cultural development is still passionately argued. The kinds of social configurations reflected in widespread complexes such as Olmec, Chavin, and Huari are as elusive as ever. There is no agreement on what conditions favor the emergence of states and empires, on the extent to which cultural development is constrained by the environment, or on how diffusion can be differentiated from convergence. The Mayan enigma remains unsolved, although several ingenious new theories have been proposed to account for the appearance and decline of this fascinating cultural configuration. If our goal is to understand the process of cultural evolution in the Americas, we have not made significant headway during the past seven years.

I was not prepared for these conclusions. When I began to reread the text, I expected many more changes would be needed than I have made. Several significant sites have been added to the maps showing the peopling of the hemisphere and the diffusion of pottery making, and the wording of a few paragraphs has been altered. Aside from these minor revisions, the story remains as valid (or invalid) as it was in 1972. Why should this be so? At least three kinds of reasons come to mind.

First, the level of generality required to compress the prehistory of the hemisphere into so few pages is too great to be affected by data that merely fill gaps in chronology, geographical distribution, and cultural inventory, or provide other details of local importance. Where I had to choose between conflicting interpretations, the choice has either proved felicitous or the issue remains unresolved.

Second, the criteria needed to resolve broad issues do not emerge from refinements in the methods of collecting and processing archeological data, which account for a significant proportion of the efforts expended during the past decade.

The third reason for this contradictory state of affairs is the most interesting and important. Many anthropologists continue to accept or are reluctant to challenge the doctrine that the acquisition of culture removed our species from the limitations placed on the activities of all other kinds of organisms by their biological constitutions and their environments. Ecological factors are considered irrelevant and population pressure is adduced to account for events as different as migrations, inventions, the domestication of plants, and the emergence of empires. Unfortunately, the archeological record can seldom be read with sufficient precision to establish whether a population increased before or after the event its growth is supposed to have caused. A more serious difficulty is that population pressure itself requires explanation.

Is our species really exempt from the complicated interplay of selective forces that integrates all other kinds of organisms into what we call "ecosystems"? Are there really no restrictions on the ways in which we can organize our societies, satisfy our requirements for food, and indulge our whims? For many natural scientists and some anthropologists, such a view is incompatible with all we have learned since evolution replaced special creation as the explanation for the origin of living things. It is also inconsistent with what we know about the way in which cultures have developed and are distributed over the earth. Even the most superficial examination of New World prehistory reveals similar kinds of cultural configurations associated with similar habitats. For example, the settlement patterns, social organizations, and many details of the material inventories characteristic of the Forest and Desert areas of North America resemble each other less than they do the counterpart region in South America. We know the environment is a major cause of convergences in the appearance and behavior of plants and animals. It therefore seems a logical candidate for explaining convergences in culture.

No science can advance without a uniform theoretical framework for evaluating evidence and constructing hypotheses. In physics, the theory of general relativity was proposed before instruments were available to examine many of its implications. Some of the latter strike the layman as outlandish, yet excitement mounts as new observations are found to be consistent with predictions, and implications long awaiting verification are found to be correct. In biology, the synthetic theory of evolution continually opens new avenues for exploration and illuminates strange behaviors and peculiar structures among animals and plants. In anthropology, by contrast, the absence of a comprehensive general framework makes it impossible to judge which facts are important and which are trivial or to distinguish correct from erroneous observations. Interpretations are accepted or rejected for any reason, however arbitrary or subjective, and the reasons become nearly as numerous as the investigators. Until this stage is superseded, we can accumulate facts endlessly but their meaning will elude us.

For those who have accepted the working hypothesis that culture is a specialized kind of behavior acted upon by natural selection to bring and maintain our species in harmony with the rest of the ecosystem, the past decade has not been devoid of exciting discoveries. These have been initiated by paleobiologists and geologists, whose increased capacity to reconstruct prehistoric environments is giving us unexpected pictures. For example, although archeologists have long been aware that conditions were different during the late Pleistocene than today, it was generally assumed the principal alteration was southward displacement of biotic communities. We have been completely wrong. Not only did most of Alaska and adjacent Siberia remain free of ice during glacial periods; this area supported a combination of flora and fauna unlike anything existing now. The "Arctic-Steppe biome" was a vast expanse of lush pasture on which herds of grazing and browsing animals that now occupy distinct habitats lived in harmony (Fig. 1).

Equally remarkable is the picture developing for the Amazon Basin. Here, the climate was cooler and dryer during glacial periods and the forest was broken by large expanses of open landscape dominated by grasses and scrubby vegetation. The composition of the fauna is not well known, but it also is likely to have differed from modern savanna communities. Knowing that the first human inhabitants lived under conditions quite different from those familiar to us provides new perspectives for assessing the archeological evidence. Perhaps the argument over man's role in the extinction of the megafauna can be settled; perhaps we can agree on whether a "Pre-Projectile Point" stage preceded the use of stone points.

Another kind of natural phenomenon that can drastically alter selective pressures and thus upset the balance of an ecosystem is a local catastrophe. Draining a lake will produce extinction of aquatic biota, reduce the abundance of shoreline species, and allow proliferation of other taxa. The eruption of a volcano can exterminate all life on a small island. Since many volcanic regions are densely inhabited, it would be surprising if eruptions had no effect on human history. One intriguing event occurred about A.D. 260, when Ilopango blanketed the highlands of southeastern El Salvador so thickly with ash that large parts of the area were rendered unfit for intensive agriculture for several generations. This disaster left its mark on flourishing Mayan settlements in the form of unfinished constructions, buried monuments, and sudden depopulation. About the same time, Classic Mayan culture crystalized in the lowlands, an environment distinct from other "cradles" of civilization. This paradox has eluded satisfactory explanation. If the highlanders sought refuge there because their mountain habitat was destroyed, however, and if they applied their considerable agricultural expertise to render productive this adopted homeland, then the situation becomes not only understandable but expectable. An ecological perspective transforms Mayan culture from an enigma to a special case of a general rule, which provides a basis for interpreting other puzzling aspects of its organization and history.

To suggest that natural selection operates on cultural behavior as it does on biological behavior is not to deny that culture has special characteristics. Rather, it puts these characteristics into a broad evolutionary context. We have a great advantage over noncultural animals. Because culture is learned, it can be unlearned, modified rapidly, and disseminated independently of biological relationships. The acquisition of culture not only freed our species from the necessity of reinventing tools and techniques, it also displaced the locus of extinction from the biological to the cultural realm. Civilizations rise and fall; people survive, adjust, and leave descendents. Or more accurately, they used to do so.

Suddenly, behavior, once so adaptive that it raised our species from obscurity to omnipotence, has become dangerous. Culture has provided us with capabilities for effecting change that far exceed our understanding of the consequences of our activities. We have power, but not control. Even worse, the forces of natural selection have been weakened by the global integration achieved during the past few decades. Whereas the prehistoric Anasazi and Tupiguaraní had to emigrate or starve when drought reduced their food supply, people similarly affected today can maintain and even increase their numbers because they are not dependent on local resources. How long can this continue? Will we repeat the history of the dinosaurs or can we cross the threshold never passed before and achieve some degree of conscious control over our collective fate?

This is the question that haunts us. No other species has acquired the capacity to interfere with the chemical, physical, and biological processes that have prevailed since the origins of terrestrial life. Yet we are products of biological evolution and part of the global ecosystem. As such, we must ultimately be affected, as many other organisms already are, by changes in the environment. If we understand our place in nature, perhaps we will be able to cope with our uniqueness and what it portends. Clues concealed in the archeological record can show us the mistakes of our predecessors as well as their accomplishments. Thousands of extinct cultures provide us with examples of many kinds of configurations. We can analyze their histories, integrations with their habitats, relationships with other societies, internal organizations, and myriad other characteristics. We can compare examples of convergence, long-term stability, and rapid change, and try to identify the conditions under which they are likely to occur.

From these investigations, we should be able to formulate a general theory of culture that will specify the extent to which it is susceptible to our conscious manipulation. This goal is far removed from the antiquarianism that gave birth to archeology, but its attainment is the most important challenge human beings have ever faced. There is no better laboratory for this task than prehistoric America.

Preface
to the First Edition

Students tend to look upon assigned research papers as distasteful chores, yet the requirement of responding to a set of arbitrary limitations can be a creative challenge. This book originated as an assignment from Unesco to summarize the archeology of the New World in 100 manuscript pages. Since more than this could easily be written on a single well-known culture or one small region, it was obvious that only a relatively high level of generalization would permit compressing the whole sweep of American prehistory into so short a space. The solution was provided by the culture area concept, adapted so as to take maximum advantage of environmental similarities between North and South America.

Being forced to look at the archeological remains in this ecological perspective brought to my attention many fascinating resemblances that I had previously overlooked. In fact, the cultural parallels between widely separated but environmentally similar regions are often extraordinary, as many of the figures clearly show. Since there is a tendency among anthropologists to discount the significance of such comparisons on the basis that they ignore a large mass of less similar data, it is worth noting that evidence cannot be selected unless it exists. Too often, cultural parallels between distant regions have been taken for granted rather than recognized as phenomena that need to be explained. It is the thesis of this book that they are neither fortuitous nor inconsequential, but an indication of the strength of environmental pressures on cultural development. Diffusion, duplicate invention, convergence, adaptation: all these are undoubtedly involved. Yet there are more fundamental questions; among them, how inevitable was the process? Are the possibilities as limited as the data appear to suggest? If so, what does this mean for mankind? Hundreds of specific situations need to be investigated before the variables can be sorted out; until the superficial aspects can be distinguished from the crucial ones, we will not have a reliable basis for interpretation. It is my hope that some of those who read what follows will be inspired or provoked to devote themselves to investigating these mysteries and in this way will not only bring us closer to a solution, but will discover and enjoy the intellectual adventure of archeology.

This volume is a revision of the Unesco article, from which it differs principally in the inclusion of information accumulated since 1967, and in the addition of a final chapter and numerous illustrations. The original version was read by a number of colleagues, whose constructive comments I wish to acknowledge with gratitude: Ripley P. Bullen, Clifford Evans, James A. Ford, Ramiro Matos Mendieta, George Metcalf, and Waldo R. Wedel. Special thanks are offered to Alexander J. Morin, who suggested this revision and improved it by skillful editing, and to George Robert Lewis, who produced most of the drawings (and threatens to present an artist's point of view on their significance one of these days).

Contents

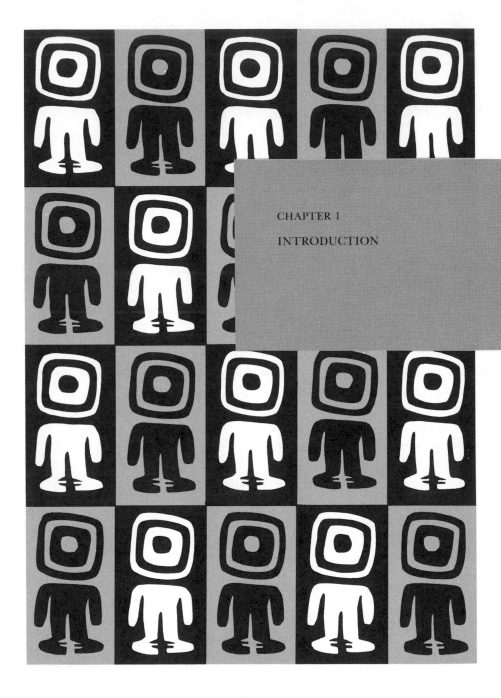

CHAPTER 1

INTRODUCTION

As a habitat for man, the New World contrasts with the Old World in several important features. It is not only a more compact area, it is more integrated geographically. Natural barriers are less severe than the Himalaya Mountains or the Sahara Desert, both in width and in traversability, and transitions are less abrupt. The Rocky Mountains of North America blend into the Sierra Madres of Mexico and Central America, which in turn merge into the Andes of South America, creating a hemispheric "backbone" that may have helped to channel faunal movements north and south. The location of the tallest mountains along the western margin of the land mass has produced similar vegetational configurations in North and South America. Both continents have lower and more ancient mountain systems in their eastern portions, as well as extensive grasslands. The coasts provide a suitable habitat for shellfish in both temperate and tropical latitudes, permitting people relying on this resource for subsistence to spread over long distances without significantly changing their mode of life. Prehistoric cultural development was influenced by the peculiarities of this environmental setting, which facilitated interaction between some regions, stimulated parallel developments in others, and left a few in isolation. The process has been a dynamic one, with climatic fluctuations and landscape modifications exerting varying effects on cultural adaptation during the millennia that man has been a resident of the New World.

An attempt to produce a coherent synthesis of aboriginal American cultural development requires a certain amount of temerity. Archeological research is progressing so rapidly that even a generalized account is vulnerable to rapid obsolescence. There is also the problem of erratic information. Whereas hundreds of thousands of pages have been published on the better known regions and large volumes are devoted to sites and complexes that cannot even be mentioned within the space of a brief review, vast expanses have yet to feel the archeologist's foot, much less his trowel. When evidence is abundant, it is often contradictory and acceptance or rejection of alternatives depends on the theoretical framework employed.

These are difficulties that archeology shares with other paleosciences, all of which must interpret their data in fragmentary form through the distorting filter of historical accident. Of the hundreds of millions of species that have evolved and become extinct, only a minute fraction is preserved in the paleontological record, and this fraction is biased by over-representation of the rigid parts of a plant or animal and of those habitats where conditions most favored fossilization. The archeologist faces the same handicap, and reconstructions of the evolution of cultures are subject to comparable limitations in accuracy. Like the paleontologist, he supplements his data with observations on living groups exhibiting a similar level of development, cognizant of the possibilities for error that this procedure involves. He can also amplify his data by evaluating them in the framework of functional and ecological theory, on the assumption that the processes guiding adaptation and evolution have not changed. Knowledge of these processes is also rudimentary, however, introducing another potential source of distortion. Fortunately, ethnologists have recently begun to take greater interest in the adaptive aspects of culture, and their findings should illuminate many puzzling features of the archeological record. Another inadequately exploited form of evidence is provided by linguistics, particularly lexicostatistical analysis and glottochronology. Since language is less susceptible to adaptive pressures than other aspects of culture, patterns of language distribution may reveal ancient connections between widely separated groups, permitting reconstruction of long forgotten population movements.

The reconstruction of prehistoric cultural development was handicapped even more before an absolute time scale became available. The discovery that carbon-14, an element present in all living things, disintegrates at a constant rate after death was a major breakthrough for New World archeology, and the thousands of carbon-14 "dates" that have been obtained during the past two decades have forced reconsideration of many earlier theories. Too often, however, it is forgotten that carbon-14 determinations are not dates in the calendrical sense, but only general approximations of age. Each result carries a plus-or-minus correction, but even this span (which may for technical reasons embrace less than 20 or more than 5000 years) has only two chances out of three of including the true age of the sample. This situation, and many other potential sources of error, makes it unsafe to base judgments about the relative antiquity of two sites or complexes on carbon-14 dates alone, particularly when the difference between dates being compared is close to their combined plus-or-minus errors.

2

Generalization requires the elimination of conflicting evidence and there are few statements in the following pages that could not be disputed by an expert on the area or culture involved. The objection can also be made that emphasis has been placed on similarities, diverting attention from the differences between each pair of areas. Nor does the fact that the data can be assembled into a consistent picture necessarily imply that it is an accurate one. Revolutionary discoveries made during the past decade have forced revision of long accepted points of view and we may expect equally drastic changes to result from investigation of the many regions still superficially known. What follows, therefore, is an impressionistic reconstruction of New World prehistory unlikely to stand the test of many years time.

This being the case, it is appropriate to ask why the effort should not be deferred until the data are more complete. There are several justifications, among them the desire to satisfy our curiosity about those who inhabited this hemisphere before us, the obligation to recognize the contribution made by American Indians to modern civilization, and the need to achieve a perspective that permits identification of the most urgent research tasks. Perhaps most significant of all, however, is the prospect of learning more about how culture operates and thereby enhancing our ability to deal rationally with our own growing social and ecological crises.

The New World is a unique anthropological laboratory because the process of aboriginal cultural development proceeded in near isolation before it came to an abrupt halt with the influx of European soldiers, priests, explorers, and colonists after A.D. 1492. In some regions, such as the Greater Antilles, the eastern United States, and the Argentine pampa, the impact was devastating and the indigenous inhabitants quickly became extinct. In others, particularly the Mesoamerican and Andean highlands, Indians continue to comprise the bulk of the rural population as they did in pre-Spanish times, but their culture has become a hybrid of indigenous and European ways. Only in a few inaccessible regions like the Amazonian forest does the aboriginal pattern persist. Where 50 million bison once roamed the North American plains, 50 million automobiles now crowd the highways. In the United States, rivers have been dammed, forests cleared, and hills leveled, so that even the landscape bears little resemblance to that of 400 or even 200 years

3

ago. The hemisphere is dominated by people who continue to trace their history through European antecedents to the ancient civilizations of the Mediterranean and the Middle East, in spite of nearly half a millennium of residence in the New World.

Yet, if we penetrate below the surface, it becomes clear that modern civilization would be a different thing without the discoveries of the American Indian. Rubber, a crucial ingredient in thousands of devices from supersonic planes to rubber bands, is a New World plant. Tobacco, which provides enjoyment to people nearly everywhere, was domesticated in the Americas. Chocolate, one of the world's most popular confections, was an Aztec beverage. Maize (corn) in a hundred varieties is the staff of life of millions of people and the source of livelihood of other millions, from cereal manufacturers and raisers of animal feed to circus popcorn venders. White potatoes have become so important in Ireland that they are commonly known as "Irish," although they were domesticated in the Andes. Cashew nuts and peanuts, avocados and pineapples, beans, squash, sweet potatoes, manioc, tomatoes, and chili peppers are among other New World plants that have been incorporated into the diet of people throughout the world. Thousands owe their health, if not their lives, to quinine and cocaine, which were discovered by South American Indians. The list could be amplified to include fibers, games, articles of furniture and dress, all of which have been so thoroughly integrated into modern civilization that we tend to forget that they are not part of our Old World heritage.

Beyond this material impact on our daily lives, New World prehistory has another contribution to make, of a more theoretical but perhaps ultimately a more significant nature. As world culture increases in complexity, its grip on mankind becomes more critical. Nations are impelled along courses over which their leaders have little control, while large populations are helpless to extricate themselves from privation and want. Our only hope is to study this amorphous phantom known as "culture," to unravel its processes of development and its behavior, and by this knowledge gain some influence over our fate.

To achieve this end, we must find out how and why things happened when and where they did, and whether each advance was a necessary prerequisite to the one that followed. For such a study, we need the New World as well as the Old World, because by examining either one

4

alone we may go wrong. For example, writing is generally assumed indispensable to the achievement of civilization, but it was unknown to the Inca, who created one of the most remarkable empires of antiquity. The wheel, another invention often cited as essential, was never a significant element in aboriginal New World culture. The Maya had the world's most accurate calendar in 1492, but lacked draft animals and iron. Careful comparison of cultural development in the two hemispheres is thus the only framework in which the crucial factors can be isolated and hypotheses about the relative significance of different environmental, social, and historical situations can be judged.

Although for purposes of general comparative analysis, the processes of cultural development in the Old and New Worlds can be considered as separate, their histories were not completely independent. It is now clear that transpacific voyagers reached the Americas; what is not so clear is how great an impact the elements that were introduced had on New World cultural development. Were plant domestication, pottery making, metallurgy, writing, and other significant traits brought by such immigrants, or were they independently invented in the Americas? The answer has important implications. If basic achievements such as these were made at least twice on this earth, they may be inherent in the evolutionary process, and if biological evolution on another planet has produced a creature comparable to man, the possibility exists that this creature has developed a culture similar to ours. If all the basic cultural elements were invented only once, however, there is no basis for assuming their inevitability. Cultural evolution on our planet would in this case very likely be unique and we could not expect it to have an extraterrestrial counterpart. Nor could we count on the regeneration of modern civilization if it were to be destroyed.

It is an ironic fact that the importance of New World archeological investigation is becoming apparent at a time when the evidence is being eliminated at an accelerating rate. In a few decades, the expansion of cities, agriculture, dams, and roads will have obliterated many important sites. The farther this process goes, the less chance there will be to reconstruct the details of New World prehistory. If the data are not collected before the record becomes too fragmentary to read with confidence, mankind will have forfeited one of the most precious keys to self-understanding.

CHAPTER 2

SETTLING THE HEMISPHERE

One of the most controversial issues in New World archeology is the time of man's arrival. Zoological and paleontological evidence conclusively eliminate the Americas as a possible setting either for human evolution or for the earliest stages of cultural development. At the upper end of the time range, there is proof that man had penetrated to the extremes of the hemisphere by 9000 B.C. Disagreement stems from sporadic, inconclusive, but tantalizing indications of man's presence scattered over the millennia between 40,000 and 12,000 years ago, which some authorities accept and others do not. The consensus has been moving gradually in recent years, however, and the earlier date tends increasingly to be viewed with ambivalence rather than rejected outright.

Whether he came 12,000 or 40,000 years ago, man entered the New World while he was still subsisting on wild animals and plants. It is taken for granted that he arrived on foot, probably at a time when sufficient sea water was impounded in the glaciers to expose a terrestrial connection between Siberia and Alaska (Fig. 1). This situation occurred whenever the sea level was lowered about 50 meters*, a condition that prevailed during at least two long intervals within the past 50,000 years. The earliest land bridge existed between about 50,000 and 40,000 years ago, and was used by various Old World species of mammals, including the caribou and the wooly mammoth, to invade the Americas. After an interval of submergence lasting some 12,000 years, the bridge reappeared between about 28,000 and 10,000 years ago. During part of this time, however, a continuous sheet of ice extended from the Atlantic to the Pacific, terminating at a latitude slightly south of the modern political boundary between Canada and the United States (Fig. 1). Some 1200 meters thick, this monstrous glacier impeded passage by man or animals for 10,000 years. During a few millennia before the eastern and western segments fused, and again after a corridor reopened, the land bridge was passable. About 10,000 years ago, the sea level had risen sufficiently to cover the Bering Strait and since that time the New World has been accessible only across water.

*One meter is equal to 39.37 inches; one kilometer equals 0.62 mile.

7

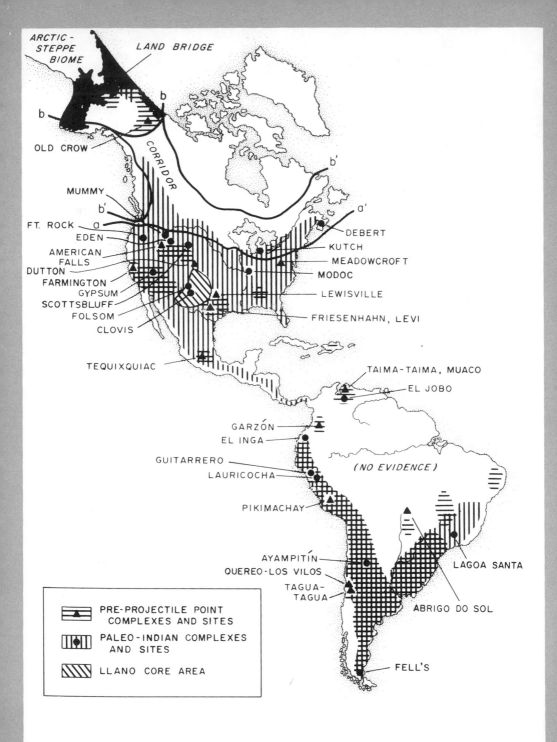

ARCTIC-
STEPPE
BIOME

LAND BRIDGE

b

b

b

OLD CROW

CORRIDOR

MUMMY

b'

FT. ROCK   a

EDEN

AMERICAN
FALLS

DUTTON

FARMINGTON

GYPSUM

SCOTTSBLUFF

FOLSOM

CLOVIS

TEQUIXQUIAC

b'

a'

DEBERT

KUTCH

MEADOWCROFT

MODOC

LEWISVILLE

FRIESENHAHN, LEVI

TAIMA-TAIMA, MUACO

EL JOBO

GARZÓN

EL INGA

GUITARRERO

LAURICOCHA

PIKIMACHAY

AYAMPITÍN

QUEREO-LOS VILOS

TAGUA-
TAGUA

(NO EVIDENCE)

LAGOA SANTA

ABRIGO DO SOL

FELL'S

PRE-PROJECTILE POINT
COMPLEXES AND SITES

PALEO-INDIAN COMPLEXES
AND SITES

LLANO CORE AREA

While many archeologists consider the Paleo-Indians to be the first Americans, others find support for the existence of earlier immigrants in the numerous sites that lack projectile points but produce large heavy choppers, scrapers, scraper-planes, knives, and hammerstones, often in remarkable abundance (Fig. 2). On the north coast of Chile, the altiplano of northwestern Argentina, and the plains of northwestern Uruguay, for example, the ground is littered for kilometers with these crude implements. In some places, such as El Jobo and Cumare in Venezuela, the artifacts occur on the highest and most distant river terrace, suggesting considerable antiquity. At Farmington, California, they are buried beneath as much as 5 meters of alluvium. At the Levi Rock Shelter in Texas, they occur stratigraphically below the earliest projectile points. Remains of mammoth, horse, sloth, camel, giant bison, tapir, dire wolf, glyptodon, and mastodon are associated in many localities, among them Friesenhahn Cavern in Texas, American Falls Reservoir in Idaho, Muaco in Venezuela, Tequixquiac in Mexico, Garzón in Colombia, and Pikimachay in Peru. At Tlapacoya, Mexico, chipped tools associated with extinct fauna have been carbon-14 dated between 24,000 ± 500 and 22,200 ± 2600 years ago. Other initial carbon-14 determinations extend from more than 37,000 years for the Lewisville site in Texas to 19,600 ± 3000 years for Pikimachay in the southern highlands of Peru, and 14,400 ± 435 years for Taima-Taima, Venezuela.

None of the finds assigned ages in excess of 24,000 years has been universally accepted by archeologists. Reasons for rejection of their

Fig. 1. *General distribution of Pre-Projectile Point and Paleo-Indian complexes and location of some representative sites. Blank areas probably reflect absence of information rather than absence of early hunters and gatherers. The Bering land bridge is shown in black. The glacial maximum, attained about 20,000 years ago, blanketed the region between lines b-b and a-a', creating a barrier that isolated the New World for several thousand years. During this time, the Arctic-Steppe biome extended from line b-b westward across the land bridge into Siberia and provided ideal resources for early hunters (see p. viii). As the ice melted, a corridor opened in western Canada, and its boundaries about 10,000 years ago are indicated by the two lines b-b'. The earliest dates and greatest concentration of sites with fluted projectile points are in the Llano core area.*

9

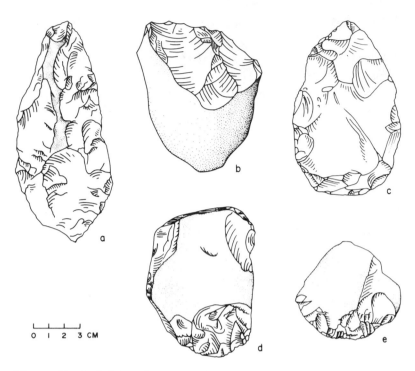

0 1 2 3 CM

Fig. 2. *Typical chipped stone artifacts from sites attributed to the Pre-Projectile Point Period. a-b, Argentina; c-e, United States.*

authenticity are varied. In some instances, the crudely chipped stones cannot be proved to be the product of human rather than natural agency; in others, the association between the carbon-14 date and the cultural remains is questioned; in still others, the antiquity of the geological context is disputed, or the artifacts are considered intrusive and consequently of more recent origin. When the evidence for a Pre-Projectile Point stage is viewed in paleoenvironmental context, however, two intriguing factors emerge that enhance its credibility. One is the existence of a land bridge prior to 37,000 years ago, which was crossed by several species of Asiatic game animals, including the caribou and mammoth. It is reasonable to suppose that conditions favorable for the prey were also favorable for the hunter. The other is the magnitude of the difference in the dates proceeding from north to south. If those now available are reliable and representative, they imply the kind of slow geographical expansion that would be in keeping with the probable small size of an initial immigrant population.

While the date of man's entry is disputed, there is general agreement that the first immigrants lived in small bands composed of related families. The men were primarily hunters, while the women probably collected edible wild plants and performed various domestic tasks, such as the preparation of hides for use as protection against wind, rain, and cold, and the weaving of baskets. Stone tools were unspecialized and the same implement often served for cutting, scraping, and pounding. The fact that shaping was generally limited to production of a working edge suggests that implements were made as needed and discarded when the immediate task was done (Fig. 2). In the vicinity of the glacial frontier, seasonal variation in food resources was probably minimal. Farther away, ecological niches must have been more diversified, and different combinations of subsistence resources would have been available. Most sites are correlated with open environments, principally grasslands, semideserts, and highland meadows, but whether this reflects greater ease of discovery or preference for a nonforest habitat is uncertain. The occurrence of a pebble tool complex in Alabama, where forests persisted during periods of glacial advance, suggests that the correlation may be fortuitous.

About 10,000 B.C., a pronounced alteration occurs in the archeological record in the form of a striking increase in the abundance of sites

11

and the appearance of new kinds of stone artifacts, among them delicately chipped projectile points. Two principal varieties have been recognized: (1) fluted Llano or Clovis points and (2) lanceolate Plano points. They reflect the advent of the Paleo-Indians or Big Game Hunters, so-called because their sites contain the bones of horse, camel, mammoth, and extinct species of bison.

The origin of the Paleo-Indians has long been a subject of speculation. Until a short time ago, it was believed that no Old World prototype existed for the Clovis and Plano points, and they were explained as New World inventions. As the Paleolithic of northern Eurasia becomes better known, however, it seems less likely that this interpretation is correct. Müller-Beck (1966) has shown that the lithic industries associated with late Mousterian and early Aurignacian occupants of the Eurasian tundra contain most of the requisite antecedents. Because the New World Llano complex exhibits many Mousteroid features, he postulates its introduction between 28,000 and 23,000 years ago, prior to isolation of North America by the maximum ice advance of the late Neopleistocene. In opposition to this hypothesis is the absence of stone projectile points south of the glacial front before about 12,000 B.C. If Paleo-Indians were in North America during the preceding 10 or 15 millennia, evidence of their presence continues to evade recognition, and the patterning of the carbon-14 dates strongly favors an entry after the reopening of the trans-Canadian corridor about 13,000 years ago.

From a center of dispersal that extends from eastern Arizona across New Mexico into northwestern Texas and northward into southern Wyoming (Fig. 1), fluted Clovis points were disseminated throughout the United States and northern Mexico, and sporadic finds reveal their adoption as far south as Tierra del Fuego. Lanceolate points are even more common and predominate in South American Paleo-Indian complexes. Bone points are also used, although their perishable nature makes their preservation rare.

When the initial dates for the North and South American occurrences are compared, the differences are remarkably small. Fluted points appear about 9500 B.C. on the North American plains and were already in use at Fell's Cave near the southern tip of South America by 9000 B.C. Lanceolate forms have been considered about a millennium more recent, but the validity of this interpretation is subject to reexamination in view of new evidence of their presence at Fort Rock Cave in Oregon before 11,000 B.C. and at Guitarrero Cave in the central Peruvian highlands about a thousand years later.

The diffusion of projectile point technology across the Americas within less than one and a half millennia has two important implications. First, it adds support to the case for a preceding Pre-Projectile Point horizon, since the rate of biological increase characteristic of hunting groups is too slow to have populated so vast a territory in so short a time. Second, it indicates the presence of a weapon of such markedly superior effectiveness to a hand-held spear that knowledge of its existence was followed by immediate adoption. The most logical candidate is the atlatl or spear thrower, which appears to be depicted in one of the earliest rock paintings in the central Peruvian highlands, where lanceolate projectile points have also been found (Fig. 3). By applying the propulsion force against the butt, the atlatl increases the range and penetration of a spear, making it a more efficient weapon for the killing of large mammals. Whereas this food resource would rarely have been accessible to Pre-Projectile Point hunters, it could now be exploited with relative ease. The consequence was the rapid emergence and dissemination of big game subsistence specialization, the hallmark of the Paleo-Indians.

The makers of Clovis fluted points selected as their primary adaptive niche the lush grasslands and wooded valleys of the North American high plains. Winters were milder and summers cooler than today, and the landscape was sprinkled with streams, ponds, and marshes. Many "kill" sites have been discovered, where mammoth, bison, camel, and horse bones are mingled with tools used to remove the hides and dismember the carcasses. Camp sites provide a greater variety of artifacts, including bone awls, needles, and spatulas; hammerstones, rubbing stones, scrapers, knives, gravers, projectile points, and more nondescript kinds of stone tools, as well as chipping debris. Although the exposed nature of Paleo-Indian sites has reduced the cultural inventory to its most durable remnants, many perishable objects were undoubtedly also in use, such as cordage, bags, and clothing of skins; mats and baskets of vegetal fibers; and ornaments of seeds, bone, and perhaps feathers. Occasional accidental finds, such as a fragment of shell engraved with a mammoth retrieved in 1891 from a Delaware peat bog,

Fig. 3. Pictograph on the wall of a rock shelter near Lauricocha in highland Peru, possibly of Paleo-Indian origin. One of the animals has been speared and the hunter holds another spear and a shorter object that may be a spear thrower.

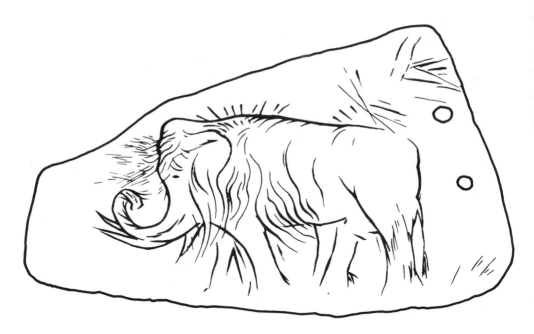

Fig. 4. Engraving of a mammoth on a piece of shell, which has been perforated at the broad end, possibly to be worn as an ornament or amulet. This object was preserved in a peat bog in Delaware and accidentally discovered in 1891.

hint tantalizingly at an artistic skill comparable to that of European Upper Paleolithic hunters (Fig. 4).

The diagnostic Paleo-Indian artifacts are the projectile points. Typical Clovis points (Fig. 5) range from 7 to 12 cm. in length, although specimens as short as 4 cm. have been found. Their width is approximately one-third to one-quarter of the length, producing an elongated outline with nearly parallel to convex sides and a concave base. Aberrant examples have slightly concave lower margins or an incipient stem resembling a fish tail. A channel or flute extending upward from the base for one-quarter to one-half the length is the diagnostic feature. On the Folsom variety, restricted to the North American plains, the major portion of each surface was removed. The "fishtailed" variant has been found in Panama, in the Ecuadorian highlands, near São Paulo in southern Brazil, and in Tierra del Fuego. Plano points are less uniform (Fig. 6), but two varieties are typical: one has parallel sides and a square base or an incipient stem; the other is a long narrow oval, tapering toward both ends. Size variation is comparable to the Clovis range and excellence of workmanship reaches its most perfect expression in the fine parallel flaking of Eden and Scottsbluff points from Wyoming and Western Nebraska.

Paleo-Indian sites are more easily recognized than those of the Pre-Projectile Point horizon, both because they have suffered less geological disturbance and because the artifacts are more striking, but their greater representation in the archeological record cannot be attributed solely to higher visibility. The acquisition of a more efficient subsistence technology must have permitted an increase in population density, which in turn would be expressed in larger numbers of sites. In habitats where large mammals were absent or uncommon, the earlier and more generalized hunting and gathering pattern probably persisted little changed. The only major region that has failed to produce either Pre-Projectile Point or Paleo-Indian remains is the Amazonian lowland, where the absence of suitable stone limited the artifact inventory to perishable objects that do not survive in the wet tropical climate. The fact that wild food resources compare favorably with those of temperate forests and the evidence that bone projectile points were part of the Paleo-Indian tool kit make it unsafe to assume that this area was avoided by early hunting and gathering peoples.

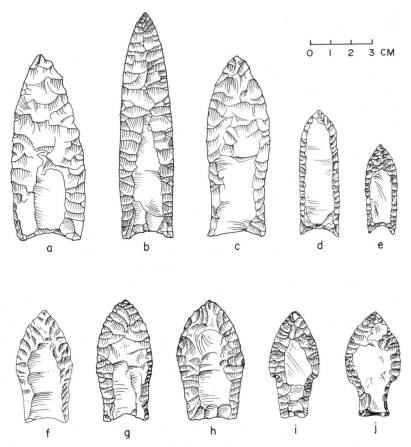

Fig. 5. *Llano or Clovis points, one of the principal Paleo-Indian types, distinguished by a channel or flute created by removal of a flake from the lower surface on one or both faces. In the Folsom variant (d-e), only the margins remain intact. a-e, United States; f, Mexico; g-h, Central America; i, Ecuador; j, southern Patagonia.*

16

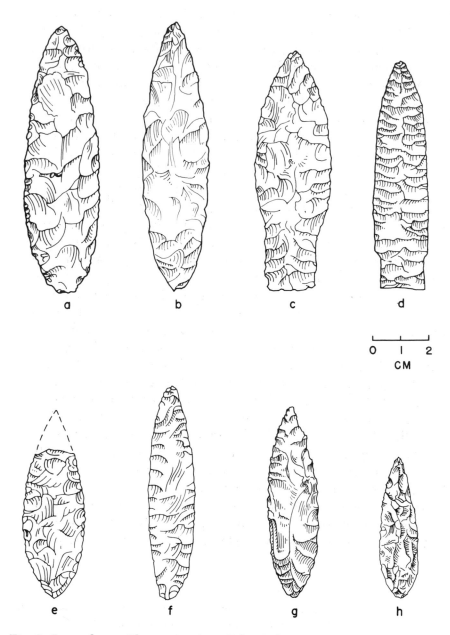

Fig. 6. *Lanceolate or Plano points from Paleo-Indian sites. a, western Siberia; b, Oregon; c-d, stemmed variant from western North America; e, Mexico; f, Venezuela; g, Peru; h, Argentina.*

As the glaciers withdrew for the last time to the north, changing ecological conditions brought extinction of many Pleistocene species, and
big game hunting could no longer serve as a major focus of subsistence
except in restricted regions such as the North American high plains.
Between about 8000 and 5000 B.C., the environment began to resemble
that of modern times, and changing conditions are reflected culturally
in the appearance of new forms of subsistence, settlement pattern, and
technology. During this Transitional Period, the sea rose to its present
level and the climate altered sufficiently to permit forests to replace
parklands and to convert formerly well-watered regions into semideserts. Environmental alterations were not equally pronounced everywhere, and ancient hunting and gathering patterns probably continued
with little or no significant alteration in many areas. Two additional
types of subsistence emphases appear to have differentiated during this
time, however, in response to increased availability of specialized local
resources: shellfish exploitation along the coasts and seed gathering in
semiarid regions (Fig. 7). Although these three categories grade into
one another and share a common denominator in material culture, in
the form of the addition of grinding and polishing to the technology of
stone working and in the substitution of a variety of stemmed projectile
points for the Paleo-Indian forms (Fig. 8), they permitted different
degrees of population concentration and sedentariness, and offered
differing potentialities for cultural evolution to a more complex level.

   The generalized hunters and gatherers, the most ancient and widespread of the three Transitional subsistence patterns, constituted a
flexible adaptation to the vast forest-covered stretches on both continents. They were generalized in the sense of relying on a variety of
wild foods, rather than in the sense that the same kinds of plants and
animals were exploited over wide areas. Both the fragmentary archeological evidence and studies of living hunting and gathering groups indicate that the total range of locally available resources was never used.

*Fig. 7. Distribution of the three principal varieties of subsistence
exploitation developed during the Transitional Period.*

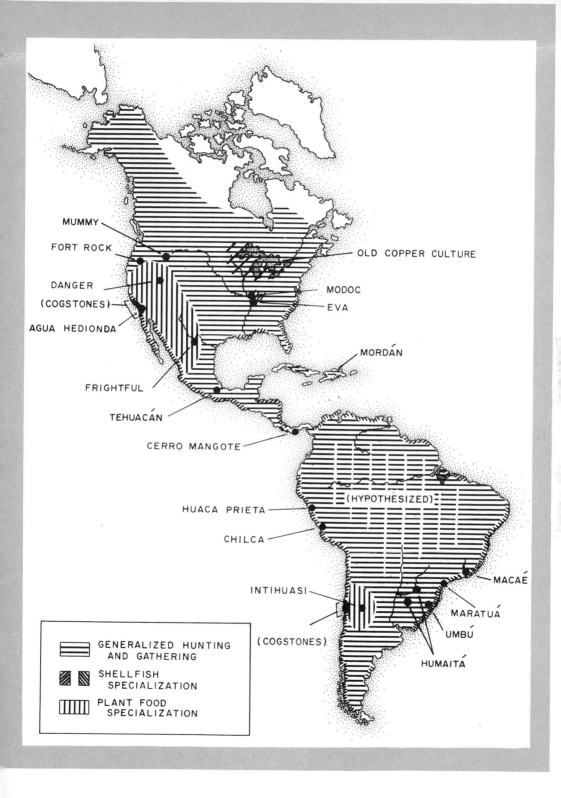

MUMMY

FORT ROCK

OLD COPPER CULTURE

DANGER

MODOC

(COGSTONES)

EVA

AGUA HEDIONDA

MORDÁN

FRIGHTFUL

TEHUACÁN

CERRO MANGOTE

HUACA PRIETA

(HYPOTHESIZED)

CHILCA

MACAÉ

INTIHUASI

MARATUÁ

UMBÚ

(COGSTONES)

HUMAITÁ

GENERALIZED HUNTING
AND GATHERING

SHELLFISH
SPECIALIZATION

PLANT FOOD
SPECIALIZATION

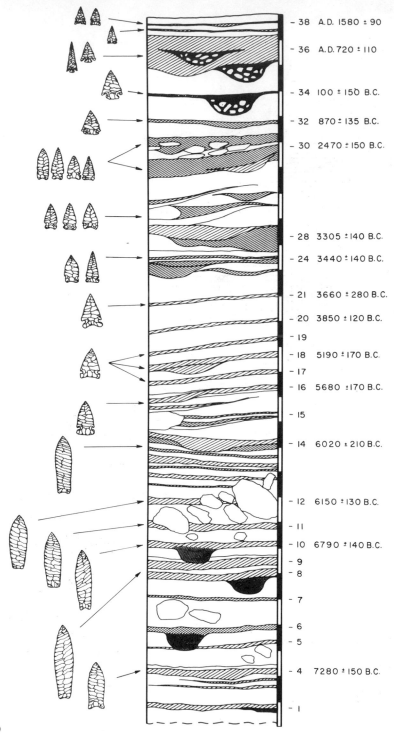

- 38   A.D. 1580 ± 90

- 36   A.D. 720 ± 110

- 34   100 ± 150 B.C.

- 32   870 ± 135 B.C.

- 30   2470 ± 150 B.C.

- 28   3305 ± 140 B.C.

- 24   3440 ± 140 B.C.

- 21   3660 ± 280 B.C.

- 20   3850 ± 120 B.C.

- 19

- 18   5190 ± 170 B.C.

- 17

- 16   5680 ± 170 B.C.

- 15

- 14   6020 ± 210 B.C.

- 12   6150 ± 130 B.C.

- 11

- 10   6790 ± 140 B.C.

- 9
- 8

- 7

- 6
- 5

- 4   7280 ± 150 B.C.

- 1

Rather, emphasis was placed on a combination that provided both a balanced diet and a reliable quantity throughout the year. The number of potential combinations permitted by forest environments is considerable, and the subsistence patterns developed during these millennia of adaptation continued to play an important role in most regions even after the adoption of agriculture, serving as a cushion against crop failure and providing nutrients lacking in cultivated plants.

The culture of the Transitional hunters and gatherers is known as the Archaic tradition in North America east of the Rockies, where it emerged between about 7000 and 5000 B.C. Complexes with similar artifact inventories occur widely in South America and are of comparable antiquity. An important technological innovation was the grinding and polishing of stone, which led to the production of new kinds of artifacts, including grooved axes, mortars and pestles, atlatl weights, plummets, and bowls. Flaking continued to be employed for making knives, scrapers, choppers, and projectile points, which proliferated into a variety of stemmed forms (Fig. 9). Frequent use of rock shelters as dwelling places has permitted survival of many otherwise perishable objects, such as bone awls, fishhooks, gouges, flutes, and beads, as well as sandals, baskets, matting, and other articles of vegetal fibers. The first burials date from this period and also the earliest evidence of the domesticated dog.

Both the location of the archeological sites and the types of tools they contain imply exploitation of a variety of foods, some available throughout the year and others seasonally. Deep accumulations of habi-

Fig. 8. Stratigraphic profile of an excavation in Mummy Cave, a rock shelter in northwestern Wyoming, exhibiting 38 distinct periods of human occupation separated by layers of sterile silt. Projectile points shown at the left change from Paleo-Indian lanceolate types to Transitional Period side-notched and stemmed forms. Carbon-14 dates on the right indicate that the Transitional Period began here about 5800 B.C. Careful analysis of deep deposits such as this provides information for the reconstruction of subsistence and settlement pattern, and also clearly establishes the chronological relationships of the various projectile point types and other kinds of artifacts.

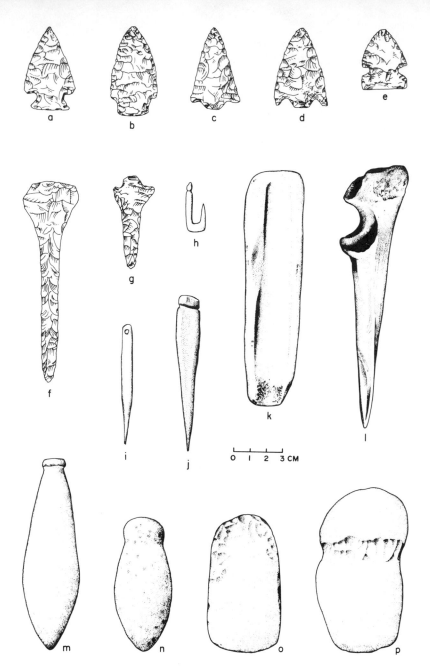

Fig. 9. Typical stone and bone artifacts of the Transitional Period. Although these are from eastern North America, similar forms occurred throughout most of the New World during this period. a-e, projectile points; f-g, drills; h, fishhook; i, needle; j, l, awls; k, gouge; m-n, plummets; o, adze; p, grooved ax.

tation refuse reveal that sheltered places favorable for winter camps were often utilized repeatedly over long periods of time; other sites produce a handful of remnants, indicating that people remained only a few days or weeks to exploit ripening berries, nuts, and other seasonal plant products, and to hunt and fish. Where preservation is good, as it is in the Tehuacán valley of central Mexico, careful analysis of the plant and animal remains has permitted reconstruction of the annual subsistence round during the sixth millennium B.C. in considerable detail (Fig. 10). During the wet season, several families congregated in places where wild maize, squash, cactus fruits, and various kinds of seeds were obtainable in abundance. When the dry season began, this macroband fragmented into smaller units, which moved about to exploit more dispersed subsistence resources. Throughout the year, about half the food intake consisted of meat, principally deer, rabbit, and iguana (MacNeish, 1967). Although the incompleteness of the archeological record necessitates a somewhat stylized reconstruction of the prehistoric way of life, the general pattern bears a close resemblance to that still followed in other parts of the Americas at the time of European contact (compare Figs. 10 and 97).

During the late Archaic, between about 2000 and 1000 B.C., the inhabitants of the Great Lakes area were unique in possessing many kinds of implements of copper as well as stone. More than 20,000 objects have been collected from the region extending over southern Saskatchewan, Minnesota, Wisconsin, Michigan, and Ontario. Copper was mined with stone tools and worked by hammering to produce a variety of artifacts (Fig. 11): tanged or socketed spear or projectile points, harpoons, adzes, celts, knives, chisels, spatulas, awls, needles, fishhooks, pikes, and beads. The origin of this industry has provoked considerable speculation. One school of thought explains it as an indigenous transfer to a new raw material of tool types and techniques of manufacture known for thousands of years; the other finds the tool shapes and hafting methods too similar to those prevalent in the Old World to have been independently invented. Whatever the origin, it is important to note that this is not a form of metallurgy. The people of the "Old Copper Culture" were simply Archaic hunters who made some of their weapons and ornaments from an unusual, locally available type of "stone."

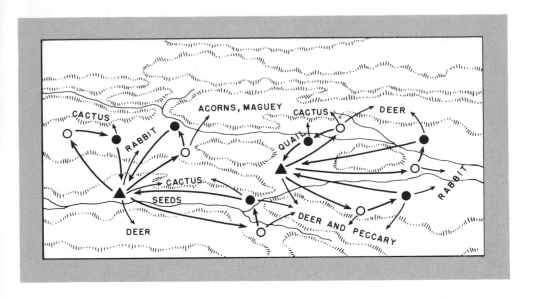

Fig. 10. *The annual subsistence cycle in the Tehuacán basin of highland Mexico between about 6800 and 5000 B.C., reconstructed from food remains in archeological sites. During the rainy season, several families could camp together (triangles), since food resources in the form of cactus fruits, seeds, wild maize, quail, and rabbits were abundant in the valley; probably periodic trips were also made to the hills to gather wild avocado and other plant products and to hunt deer. In the fall, families separated and moved in different directions (open circles) to exploit more dispersed resources, such as acorns and maguey available on the higher slopes. As the dry season progressed, camp was moved again (black circles); while sparser foliage made deer and peccary easier to hunt, plant foods became rarer and one of the mainstays appears to have been cactus leaves. This general way of life is very similar to that prevalent among Marginal peoples at the time of European contact (cf. Fig. 97).*

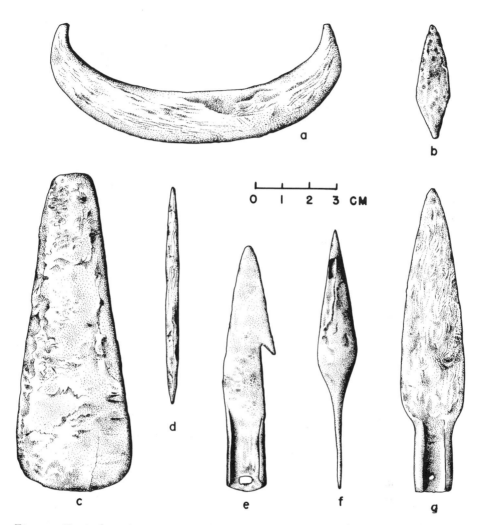

Fig. 11. *Typical artifacts of the Old Copper Culture, which existed in the Great Lakes region between about 2000 and 1000 B.C. a, knife; b, projectile point; c, celt; d, awl; e, harpoon point; f, tanged spear point; g, socketed spear point.*

In the semiarid western United States, a more specialized subsistence pattern emphasizing wild plants began to take shape about 8000 B.C. (Fig. 7). Sites representing this "desert culture" are distributed over much of western North America, between Oregon and central Mexico. In some regions, acorns, piñon nuts, grass seeds, edible roots, and berries provided an abundant annual harvest; in others, resources were less prolific and more scattered. South American sites of the desert culture are poorly known, but excavations at Intihuasi cave in northwestern Argentina attest to the presence of a similar subsistence adaptation by 6000 B.C. Although the abundance of projectile points implies that hunting continued to be important, the hallmarks of this way of life are baskets for the gathering of seeds and berries and milling stones for removing hard shells and pulverizing seeds into flour. The annual cycle was regulated by the seasonal maturation of seeds and fruits, and many groups probably followed a rather fixed schedule, moving from place to place as different types of wild crops reached maturity. In parts of the Great Basin, coastal California, and northern Mexico, this subsistence pattern remained viable until the end of the aboriginal period, and ethnographic accounts of the Paiute, Shoshone, and other tribes whose material culture resembles that found in ancient desert culture sites provide a glimpse of social and religious practices probably also little changed for thousands of years.

As wandering bands of foragers filtered over the continents, they may have initially paid little attention to the subsistence possibilities along the shores. When the extinction of the horse, mammoth, and other Pleistocene big game made hunting less productive, however, the bountiful supply of shellfish available along many parts of the Atlantic and Pacific coasts began to be exploited (Fig. 7). Shell middens of fantastic dimensions on the coasts of Peru, Chile, southern Brazil, and the southeastern United States are mute testimony to the productivity of this subsistence resource. Although other kinds of wild foods continued to be consumed, and shellfish gathering may often have been a seasonal activity, the ability to obtain a reliable food supply indefinitely from a restricted area permitted the shellfish gatherers to be significantly more sedentary than contemporary groups dependent upon more transitory kinds of wild food resources.

Determination of the date when specialized shellfish gathering was adopted is complicated by fluctuations in sea level during the terminal Pleistocene. Along eastern North America, for example, the shore was in some places 150 kilometers to the east of its present location when the ice sheet reached its maximum extent. Although differences in slope of the continental shelf reduce the amount of recently inundated land on the Pacific side, the present coastal configuration there too has an antiquity of only about 5000 years. This change in sea level may account for the clustering of the earliest carbon-14 dates for shell middens throughout the Americas: 5853 ± 150 B.C. for Maratua, Brazil; 5020 ± 300 B.C. for Chilca, Peru; 4850 ± 100 B.C. for Cerro Mangote, Panama; and 5320 ± 120 B.C. for southern California. The earliest date yet secured pushes back this way of life to 7070 ± 500 B.C. at Agua Hedionda in southern California. Exploitation of freshwater shellfish is of similar antiquity, to judge from a date of 5200 ± 500 B.C. from the Eva site on the Tennessee River.

Most shell middens are in regions of moist climate, and rainwater percolating through the shells has destroyed all but the most durable cultural remains. What survives consists principally of broken stones that must have served for scraping, cutting, and pounding; fish and animal bones with sharpened ends for punching or perforating, and bits of shell fashioned into beads, small amulets, or fishhooks. Polished stone implements occur in many sites, as well as zoomorphic or peculiar objects of no obvious utility that may have had a ceremonial function. The abundance of cordage, netting, basketry, matting, wooden objects, and other perishable remains in coastal Peruvian sites indicates that the material culture of these people was considerably less impoverished than the surviving inventory tends to suggest. Some of the earliest evidence of concern for the dead comes from shell middens, in the form of graves lined with red ocher and furnished with a few simple ornaments or tools.

Two small coastal regions, one in southern California and the other in central Chile (Fig. 7), have produced several hundred examples of a peculiar type of artifact known as a "cogged stone." The name comes from the characteristic California form, which is a disk with 3 to 22 grooves or indentations on the edge giving the general appearance of a cog (Fig. 12). Diameter varies between 4.5 and 15.5 cm. and thickness is between 1.0 and 6.5 cm. Some are of soft mudstone or lime-

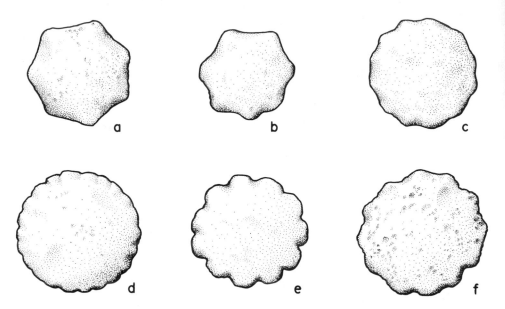

Fig. 12. Cogstones from central Chile (a-c) and southern California (d-f). Hundreds of similar objects have been found in both regions, where they are restricted to a small area and an early time period. The range of forms is much greater in Chile, but in neither area do any of the examples show traces of wear indicative of their use.

stone, others of basalt or granite. In California, distribution is restricted to the Los Angeles-San Diego area and to sites dating between about 6000 and 3500 B.C. Associated artifacts include milling stones, hammerstones, choppers, scrapers, and large projectile points, often with contracting stems. Chilean cogstones have the same range in size but are more varied in form; in addition to grooved or toothed disks, there are triangles, quadrangles, and polygons with 24 or more facets. The material is always granité. Distribution in Chile is restricted to the province of Coquimbo and to sites earlier than 1500 B.C. The associated artifact complex resembles that in California. None of the examples exhibits any damage or wear from use and they have consequently been assigned a ceremonial function. Although an introduction from one area to the other seems unlikely, convergence appears equally improbable unless the objects had some function intimately related to cultural adaptation in these two widely separated regions. In the latter event, solving the cogstone mystery would significantly advance our understanding of the limitations within which culture evolves.

PLANT DOMESTICATION

In one or more regions, adaptation to changing subsistence resources during the Transitional Period apparently involved rudimentary methods of conserving and increasing the yields of several kinds of wild plants. Incipient domestication was underway in the Mexican highlands by about 7000 B.C. and progress during the following three millennia is implied by an increase from 30 to 66 percent in the ratio of plant to animal remains in the habitation refuse of dry caves (MacNeish, 1967). Domesticated species, principally maguey, squash, avocado, and maize, account for nearly 40 percent of this increase. Although common beans and lima beans appear to have been cultivated in Peru during the seventh millennium B.C., wild foods seem to have remained the primary subsistence source in the Andean Area until the introduction of maize about 4000 B.C. (Fig. 13).

Most New World cultigens are different from those of Old World origin, but we do not yet know whether their domestication was the independent result of a similar sequence of incidents or whether the idea spread from a single world center and was applied to local plants.

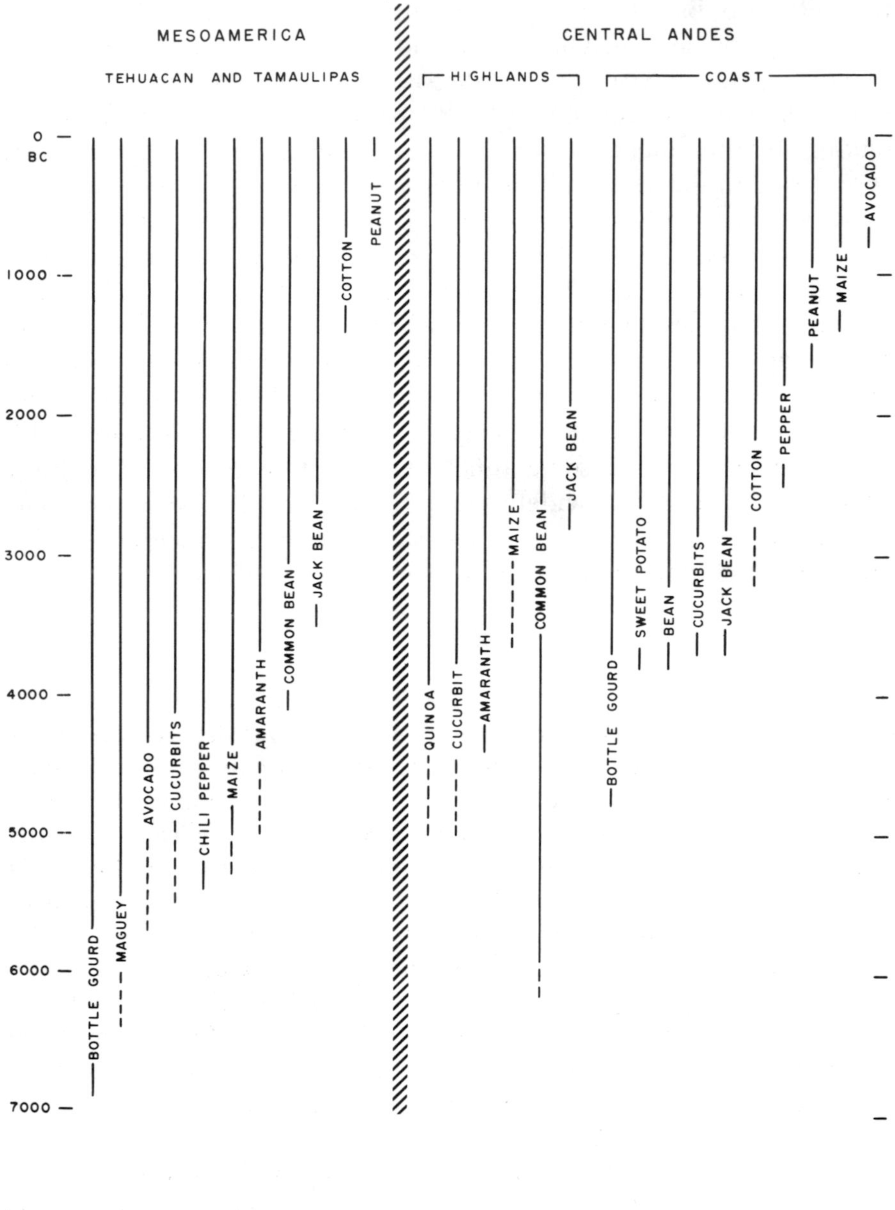

MESOAMERICA

CENTRAL ANDES

TEHUACAN AND TAMAULIPAS

HIGHLANDS

COAST

0 BC

1000

2000

3000

4000

5000

6000

7000

BOTTLE GOURD

MAGUEY

AVOCADO

CUCURBITS

CHILI PEPPER

MAIZE

AMARANTH

COMMON BEAN

JACK BEAN

COTTON

PEANUT

QUINOA

CUCURBIT

AMARANTH

MAIZE

COMMON BEAN

JACK BEAN

BOTTLE GOURD

SWEET POTATO

BEAN

CUCURBITS

JACK BEAN

COTTON

PEPPER

PEANUT

MAIZE

AVOCADO

Even within the New World, it is not yet established whether the initial steps toward agriculture that have been detected in Peru were independent of those in Mesoamerica or stimulated by Mesoamerican contact. In fact, the only real certainties are that the period of incipient domestication was a long one and that for many millennia the effects of this new food source on population size and sociopolitical organization were slight.

One of the arguments against an independent origin for New World agriculture is the fact that the earliest domesticated species, the bottle gourd *(Lagenaria)*, has no known wild ancestor in the Americas. Although some varieties are edible, it is generally cultivated for its bottle-shaped fruits, useful as containers. Rinds appear in archeological sites in northern Mexico between 7000 and 5000 B.C. and on the coast of Peru after about 5000 B.C. Another important New World domesticate, cotton, also has Old World antecedents. Although the Mexican and Peruvian cultivated species are different (*Gossypium hirsutum* in Mexico and *G. barbadense* in Peru), both are 26-chromosome hybrids. One ancestor is a 13-chromosome Old World species and the other a 13-chromosome New World species. The manner in which this hybridization came about is disputed. Some botanists trace it back to the time when the ancestral plants had a continuous distribution over the earth, long before man appeared on the scene. Others suggest a natural or artificial (that is, man-carried) transoceanic introduction of seeds, the progeny of which then crossed with a wild New World relative.

Even if Old World influence is accepted to account for the domestication of these two plants, it would not necessarily rule out the independence of New World subsistence agriculture. Indeed, the fact that the initial cultigens varied in different regions implies that the concept of·assisting nature to provide a more reliable and prolific food supply

Fig. 13. Comparison of the dates of domestication of some of the major New World staples in Mesoamerica and Peru. Many local plants were also domesticated in both regions, and others continued to be gathered, so that the vegetal diet was much more varied than this chart suggests.

was the outgrowth of a gradually increased knowledge of plant lore and a series of lucky accidents, such as favorable mutations or natural hybrids. Furthermore, recent investigations in Mexico and Peru have revealed a gradual progression from full dependence on wild foods to primary dependence upon agriculture that appears to represent an indigenous evolutionary process.

Most of the information we possess on the incipient agricultural period in Mexico has been obtained from a series of excavations in dry rock shelters in Tamaulipas and the valley of Tehuacán (Fig. 21). Among the earliest plants to figure prominently in the archeological record are mesquite, maguey, cucurbits, avocados, chili peppers, amaranth, and maize. In the case of mesquite and maguey, wild and domesticated plants are indistinguishable morphologically, so that their status as cultigens is problematic. Seeds of domesticated cucurbits (squash, pumpkin, gourd) and beans are readily identifiable, however, and their presence is clear evidence of incipient agriculture. The avocado is particularly significant because it requires more moisture than exists in the Tehuacán valley during the dry season and cannot grow there naturally. Its inclusion in the diet thus implies that irrigation, which was crucial to the expansion of agriculture in the Mexican highlands, was beginning to develop.

The origin of maize, which became the principal staple over much of the New World, has long been disputed. Of three possible ancestors —extinct wild maize, *Tripsicum,* and teosinte—botanists tend to favor the latter, which is endemic to Mesoamerica. Archeological investigations in the Tehuacán valley again provide the most complete information. Domestication began around 5000 B.C. and millennia of selective breeding increased the size of the cobs from an original length of under two centimeters and deprived the plant of the ability to reproduce without human aid. A large number of varieties were produced, differing not only in size, color, and subsistence properties, but also in viability under different conditions of moisture, temperature, soil, and length of growing season. Amaranth, another seed plant, began to be exploited about the same time.

Addition of the common bean to the diet about 4000 B.C. was an achievement of special significance because of certain biochemical circumstances. Although maize, like other grains, is high in protein, it is deficient in lysine, an enzyme essential for efficient protein metabolism by *Homo sapiens.* It so happens that beans have a high lysine content. The combination of maize and beans provides a significantly more nourishing diet than does either food alone. The maize-bean combination had two other important aspects: (1) it could be made increasingly productive through selective breeding of the plants and technological advances like irrigation and (2) it reduced dependence on wild animal **protein, which was vulnerable to overexploitation and thus placed a low** ceiling on population density. In the Tehuacán valley, these benefits are reflected in a decline in the proportion of animal foods in the diet from about 34 percent prior to bean domestication to about 17 percent in late prehistoric times (MacNeish 1967–).

The record in the Andean Area is less complete, but recent investigations in dry rock shelters indicate that the transition from gathering to incipient agriculture was earlier than previously believed. Fully domesticated common beans and lima beans have been identified in Guitarrero Cave refuse dating at least 6000 B.C. Amaranth, quinoa, and a cucurbit were under cultivation in the southern highlands by 4500 B.C., but maize and jack beans appear not to have been added to the agricultural inventory until more than a millennium later. When white potatoes and other tubers were domesticated is still uncertain. On the coast, where the evidence is both fuller and more accurately dated, a number of plants appear almost simultaneously about 3750 B.C., the most important being the common bean, the jack bean, cucurbits, sweet potatoes, jiquima, and guavas. Peanuts were introduced about 1650 B.C., maize about 1400 B.C., and the avocado a few centuries prior to the Christian era. Throughout the Andes, animal protein remained an important part of the diet as a consequence of the domestication of llamas and guinea pigs and of the productivity of the sea. By 2000 B.C., agriculture was sufficiently developed to support sedentary life in the highlands as well as on the coast, and (as happened in Mesoamerica) the appearance of impressive ceremonial structures about this time reflects both the security and the uncertainty of the new subsistence pattern.

When the Mesoamerican and Andean histories of plant domestication are compared, it is evident that a number of species are duplicated. Present knowledge places most of them earlier in Mexico than in Peru, the common bean and cotton being notable exceptions. In the Andean Area, the transition seems to have been slower on the coast than in the highlands, where conditions may have been more favorable and where most of the ancestral forms occur. Plants native to only one continent or Nuclear area (such as maize and peanuts) must have been disseminated to other regions by human agency, but some widespread cultigens (such as cucurbits) may have been domesticated independently in different places and times from the same or closely related wild ancestors.

Since the Mexican and Andean highlands have temperate to sub-tropical climates, many plants domesticated there were suitable for adoption in temperate regions to the north and south. As a result, maize, beans, and squash became staples from northeastern North America to central Chile before European contact. In the humid tropical low-lands of Central and South America, however, they were less productive and emphasis was placed on root crops, which are more tolerant of poor soils and heavy rainfall. Manioc is particularly interesting because varieties differ in the amount of hydrocyanic acid concentrated in the tubers. Those that can be eaten boiled or roasted like potatoes are termed "sweet"; those that are mildly poisonous to lethal are designated as "bitter." In spite of its potential danger, bitter manioc has certain qualities that make it a more important staple, and several techniques for elimination of the poison were developed aboriginally. Unfortunately, there is no evidence of when and where this occurred. Presumably the sweet variety was exploited first, since it requires no special treatment. Bitter manioc is often processed into flour, which is baked into a large thin wafer, and griddles utilized in this method of preparation begin to appear in archeological sites on the north coast of Colombia about 1000 B.C. This is obviously a terminal date, representing the successful culmination of several millennia of experimentation. The locus of domestication of the sweet potato, another staple of the tropical lowlands, is even more speculative and unless pollen analysis proves fruitful, its origin is unlikely ever to become known.

THE ORIGIN AND SPREAD OF POTTERY MAKING

Although pottery is not a cultural element of primary significance from the standpoint of adaptation or survival, it assumes a major role in

34

archeological investigations for three principal reasons: (1) it is too delicate and unwieldy to be easily portable and thus constitutes a reliable indicator of the adoption of sedentary life; (2) it is capable of extraordinary variation without loss of functional utility, making it a sensitive index of cultural relationship and of changing social complexity; and (3) it is second only to stone in durability, with the result that it is the principal surviving cultural evidence in many parts of the Americas. Tracing the distribution of distinctive varieties of vessel shape and decoration through time and space serves as a basis for the reconstruction of paths of diffusion and the recognition of significant advances in level of social development.

Because it is poorly suited to a mobile way of life, pottery making is usually associated with agricultural subsistence. In the New World, however, it appears earliest in coastal shell middens, at a time when plant domestication was still at an incipient stage in the Mesoamerican and Andean highlands. Since shellfish is one of the few natural food resources of sufficient permanence and concentration to substitute for agriculture as a basis for settled life, this context is not surprising. What is somewhat unexpected is the evidence that the best made and most elaborately decorated pottery, that associated with the Valdivia culture of coastal Ecuador, is also the oldest, with an initial carbon-14 date of 3200 ± 150 B.C. Large rounded bowls and small short-necked jars often have well polished surfaces and are decorated by incision, excision, punctation, rocker stamping, and other plastic techniques. Both the level of technical competence in manufacturing and the variety of the ornamentation indicate that Valdivia pottery is the culmination of a long period of development.

While our knowledge of New World prehistory is still far from complete, the emerging pattern contains no gap of sufficient magnitude to accommodate an undiscovered ancestral tradition. More significantly, the Valdivia ceramic complex (Fig. 14) resembles to a remarkable degree Middle Jomon pottery being manufactured around 3000 B.C. in Japan, particularly on the island of Kyushu (Fig. 15). In contrast to the coastal Ecuadorian sites, Japanese shell middens provide a continuous record of ceramic evolution from simple beginnings about 7000 B.C. to the well developed Middle Jomon complex. The contrast between this long archeological record and the absence of New World

Fig. 14. *Typical decorated pottery from the Valdivia culture of coastal Ecuador. a, excision; b, fingernail punctation, c-d, rocker stamping; e-g, multiple drag-and-jab; h, crude zig-zag incision; i, row of punctations at the lower margin of an incised zone; j, crosshatch; k, combination of crosshatch at rim, horizontal incision on neck and zig-zag on body; l, nicked rim; m, zoned punctation and incision; n, fingertip grooving with nicking on the intervening ridges; o-q, combing; r, interlocking incised design; s-u, broad-line incision with a square-ended tool; v, folded-over rim.*

Fig. 15. Typical decorated pottery from the Middle Jomon culture of western Japan. a, excision; b, fingernail punctation; c-d, rocker stamping; e-f, multiple drag-and-jab; g, crude zig-zag incision; h, row of punctations at the lower margin of an incised zone; i, crosshatch; j, combination of crosshatch at rim, horizontal incision on neck, and zig-zag incision on body; k, nicked rim; l, zoned punctation and incision; m-n, fingertip grooving with nicking on the intervening ridges; o-q, combing; r, interlocking incised design; s-u, broad-line incision with a square-ended tool; v, folded-over rim.

antecedents for Valdivia pottery, the striking similarity between the Middle Jomon and early Valdivia ceramic complexes, and the contemporaneity of their dates all support the conclusion that Valdivia pottery is the result of a transpacific introduction from western Japan.

During the subsequent millennium, pottery making spread to other shellfish-gathering communities (Fig. 16). At Puerto Hormiga on the Caribbean coast of Colombia, a complex incorporating several distinctive Valdivia features has been dated at 3090 ± 70 B.C. The Orange and Stallings Island ceramics of Florida and Georgia, which make their appearance about 2500 B.C., also have incised and punctate decoration indicative of an Ecuadorian origin (Fig. 17). Less information is available from the shores of Central America and Mexico, but the existence of pottery at Puerto Marquez by 2400 B.C. indicates that an early diffusion current also passed along the Pacific coast. The Monagrillo complex of Panama, dated about 2100 B.C., exhibits decorative elements consistent with a derivation from earlier representatives of the shell-midden ceramic tradition.

This tradition also appears to have spread eastward along the coast of South America. Carbon-14 dates from shell middens on the north coast of Brazil indicate that simple pottery tempered with crushed shell was being manufactured there by about 3000 B.C. Similar ceramics from shell middens of the Alaka Phase in northwestern Guyana provide a link between the Brazilian Mina Phase and the Caribbean coast of Colombia.

Although the occurrence of Valdivia-like motifs on decorated gourds from Guañape indicates there was communication with Ecuador much earlier, pottery making did not begin on the Peruvian coast until about 1750 B.C. Perhaps the greater ease of manufacture and durability of gourd vessels, which abound in the refuse of preceramic sites, impeded the adoption of pottery containers.

Fig. 16. Spread of pottery making in the New World as indicated by existing carbon-14 dates. Arrows show the directions of diffusion suggested by the increasing recency of the dates, which are oldest in shell middens along the coasts. Adoption inland was inhibited in most regions until plant domestication was sufficiently advanced to support sedentary life. Although it is possible to derive the Middle and South American ceramic traditions from a single interaction sphere, pottery characteristic of eastern North America is so different as to imply an independent introduction from Asia or Europe.

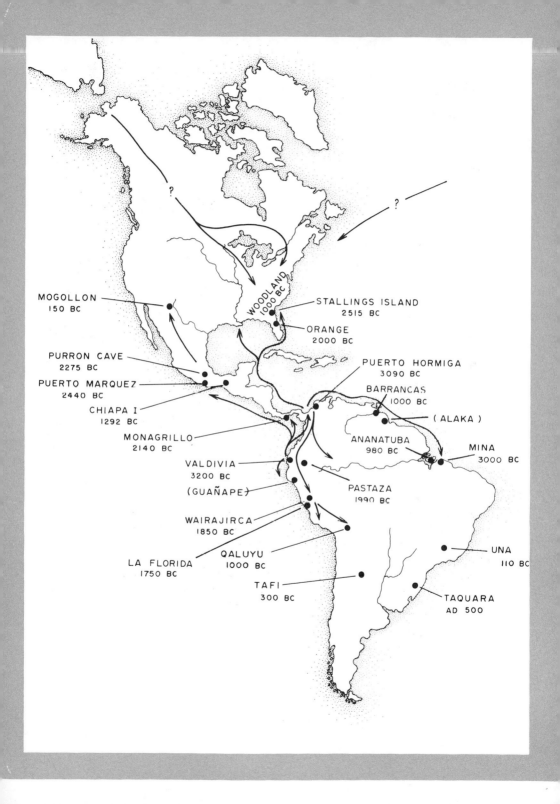

MOGOLLON
150 BC

STALLINGS ISLAND
2515 BC

ORANGE
2000 BC

WOODLAND
1000 BC

PURRON CAVE
2275 BC

PUERTO MARQUEZ
2440 BC

CHIAPA I
1292 BC

PUERTO HORMIGA
3090 BC

BARRANCAS
1000 BC

(ALAKA)

MONAGRILLO
2140 BC

ANANATUBA
980 BC

MINA
3000 BC

VALDIVIA
3200 BC

PASTAZA
1990 BC

(GUAÑAPE)

WAIRAJIRCA
1850 BC

LA FLORIDA
1750 BC

QALUYU
1000 BC

UNA
110 BC

TAFI
300 BC

TAQUARA
AD 500

a
f
b
g
c
h
d
i
e
j
Stallings Island
Valdivia

a
e
b
f
c
g
d
h
Machalilla
i
Orange
Valdivia

Fig. 17. Comparison of pottery decoration from early shell middens on the Florida (Orange Culture) and Georgia (Stallings Island Culture) coasts with that from the Valdivia and Machalilla complexes of coastal Ecuador. These resemblances, the slope in initial carbon-14 dates, as well as the similarity in subsistence and settlement pattern, indicate that the earliest North American pottery was derived by coastwise diffusion from northern South America.

40

Inland diffusion of pottery making was precluded in most regions until the domestication of plants had progressed sufficiently to support a sedentary way of life. The adoption of pottery by residents of the Tehuacán valley of highland Mexico before the second millennium B.C. thus corroborates the botanical evidence of increasing agricultural productivity; the same implication can be drawn from its presence in the Peruvian highlands about 1850 B.C. With the passage of time, local styles proliferated and influenced one another, leading to the appearance of new vessel shapes and decorative techniques, which were in turn diffused to near and distant regions.

While most later New World ceramic complexes probably evolved from the early shell-midden tradition, Woodland pottery of the eastern United States incorporates so many distinct features that an independent derivation is likely. Whereas pottery elsewhere was usually made by coiling, Woodland vessels were constructed by the paddle and anvil technique, which consisted of beating the exterior surface with a wooden paddle while the interior was supported by an anvil stone. The paddle was often wrapped with cord or a piece of cloth, which left its imprint on the clay surface; in later times, the paddle was carved so as to produce a complicated overall design. Simple, conical-based, wide-mouthed jars are the characteristic vessel form. The presence of these features in ceramics of mainland Asia suggests an introduction via the Bering Strait, but suitably ancient pottery-producing sites along the presumed route of transmittal across Canada have not yet been discovered. Another possibility is intrusion from northern Europe, where similar ceramics were being made during the second millennium B.C. Which of these is the correct explanation remains to be determined.

THE ENVIRONMENTAL CONTEXT OF LATER CULTURAL DEVELOPMENT

During the Transitional Period, the interaction of climatic, topographic, geological, and biological factors crystallized a number of major ecological areas in the Americas. By about 2000 B.C., these different sets of conditions had brought into being an equal number of highly integrated and well adapted cultural configurations, whose properties exerted a significant effect on subsequent local development. In the Central

41

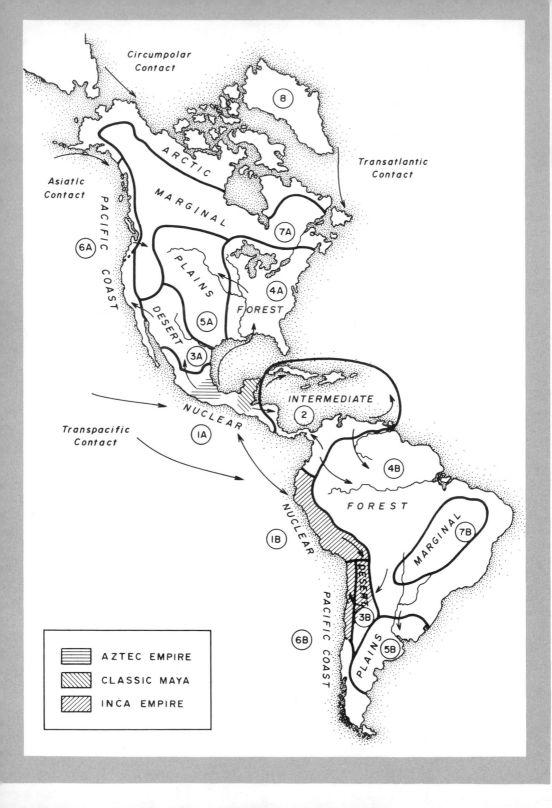

Andes and Mesoamerica, agriculture was sufficiently reliable to permit village life, establishing a foundation that was ultimately able to support urban civilization. In most other parts of the hemisphere, however, wild foods remained the sole basis of subsistence for additional centuries or millennia, and influences were accepted rapidly, slowly, or not at all depending not only on their intensity but also on their compatibility with long established local practices and beliefs.

Because New World anthropologists usually confine their attention to one continent or a portion thereof, the prehistory of North and South America has seldom been compared. When the entire hemisphere is viewed in ecological perspective, however, it becomes apparent that all but one of the major North American environmental areas have a South American counterpart (Fig. 18). This situation provides a convenient framework within which to review New World cultural development subsequent to 2000 B.C. Description will begin with the Nuclear Areas, which alone achieved a high level of civilization in pre-European times. The remaining regions will be considered in the approximate order of the decreasing complexity of their climax cultures, beginning with the Intermediate or Circum-Caribbean Area, followed by the Forests, the Deserts, the Plains, the Pacific Coasts, and the Marginals. Only the Arctic has no South American parallel. In each dichotomy, the North American member is better known archeologically and will be described first. Similarities in subsistence adaptation and cultural content will be stressed, but significant differences will also be noted. Except for the Nuclear Areas, environmentally comparable regions were isolated from one another geographically so that no direct communication is likely to have occurred between them. Consequently, they provide a unique opportunity to examine the extent to which environmental similarity influences cultural development.

Fig. 18. Major New World environmental and cultural areas. Similar habitats occur in North and South America and the close relationship between environment and cultural development is attested by similarities in the evolutionary sequences and in the general character of the climax configurations in each pair of areas. The arrows indicate the principal directions of diffusion and the major foci of extracontinental influence.

43

CHAPTER 3

CULTURAL DEVELOPMENT IN NUCLEAR

AMERICA AND THE INTERMEDIATE AREA

Civilization evolved aboriginally in two geographically separated but environmentally similar parts of the New World: Mesoamerica and the Central Andes. In both regions, priority in the transition from wild to domesticated subsistence dependence afforded a head start, and cultural development increasingly out-distanced that elsewhere in the Americas during subsequent millennia. The patterning of change followed a parallel course, channeled by similar adaptive pressures and opportunities, and influenced by the interchange of a variety of cultural elements throughout the prehistoric period. While the effects of this intercommunication must not be underestimated, the achievement of civilization cannot be attributed primarily to its stimulation. The fact that the Intermediate Area, which has a predominantly tropical climate, failed to reach an equally high level of cultural complexity in spite of continuous exposure to influences from both Nuclear Areas argues forcefully for the interpretation that environment was the more significant variable.

THE NUCLEAR AREAS

Environmental diversity is an outstanding characteristic of two New World regions. One is Mesoamerica, anthropologically defined as extending from northern Mexico to central Honduras and Nicaragua; the other is the Andean Area, corresponding in general to highland and coastal Ecuador, Peru, and Bolivia. In both, the cordilleras diverge to create intermontane basins of temperate climate, drained by non-navigable rivers running through deep tropical gorges. The higher elevation of the Andean basins is compensated by their lower latitude, so that the climate of Cuenca in the south Ecuadorian highlands, with an average annual temperature of 14° C., is comparable to that of Mexico City with an annual average of 15° C. Annual rainfall averages are also of similar magnitude: 862 mm. for Cuenca and 500–1000 mm. for Mexico City. The eastern mountain slopes, extending to the sea in Mesoamerica and to the Amazon basin in South America, are covered with dense tropical forest, while the western lowlands suffer from aridity. This juxtaposition of ecological zones with differing resource potentials for human exploitation led to regional specialization and the development of exchange networks, initiating a pattern of economic interdependence that provided a foundation for subsequent political integration.

Although the environmental ingredients are generally similar, they are combined in different proportions and arrangements in the two regions that compose Nuclear America. Mesoamerica tends to be a patchwork of mountains, basins, and valleys, bordered on the east by swampy lowlands. Semideserts, parklands, scrub forests, savannas, and tropical forests provide habitats for the most diversified mammalian fauna in the New World. At certain seasons, lakes and lagoons support migratory waterfowl in abundance. Perhaps the most significant aspect of Mesoamerican geography, however, is the relatively gradual nature of transitions in elevation, temperature, and rainfall. The result is variety without sharp contrast, facilitating the diffusion of cultural elements from one region to another.

In the Andean Area, environmental zones are larger and extremes are more marked. True deserts of barren sand on the coast contrast with perennially dripping cloud forests high on the eastern slopes of the cordillera. Frigid highland plains occur within a few kilometers of deep narrow gorges filled with tangled tropical growth. Subsistence techniques suitable to one habitat are not equally applicable to another. Vegetation is particularly sensitive to differences in elevation, temperature, and moisture as marked as those prevailing in the highlands and on the coast, so that many cultigens adapted to one of these regions were poorly suited to the other. The Andes had an advantage, however, in the existence of animals suitable for domestication, and the llama and guinea pig began to play an important role in the economy at an early time.

Until recently it was believed that the two hearths of New World civilization, Mesoamerica and the Central Andes, had achieved their development independently or at best with minimal communication. More detailed knowledge of the cultural sequences in both areas has made it increasingly evident, however, not only that a great deal of interchange took place but that it began at a relatively early time. During the early Formative Period, traits of basic significance passed from one region to the other, including pottery making and certain species of domesticated plants. Beginning shortly before the Christian era and continuing to the time of the Spanish Conquest, evidence of contact is

46

more abundant, perhaps reflecting planned trading expeditions. Flat and cylindrical stamps, small pottery masks, and numerous features of costume, ritual, and art (Figs. 19 and 20) are among elements introduced to the coast of Ecuador from Mexico, while the figurine mold, shaft-and-chamber tomb construction, and metallurgy are a few of the traits that moved from south to north. Such surviving evidence must represent a small reflection of the total cultural exchange between the two Nuclear Areas, most of which would have assumed perishable or intangible form.

Mesoamerica (Fig. 18, Area 1A). During the millennium between 2000 and 1000 B.C., the pattern of village life still prevailing in rural Mesoamerica became established throughout the highlands and on the Veracruz, Chiapas, and Guatemala coasts. Shallow, flat-bottomed bowls and globular jars (tecomates) of pottery came into general use and were often decorated with red rims and zones of brushing, punctuation, or rocker stamping. The abundance of small pottery figurines suggests that they lost their significance and were discarded after brief use, perhaps in a curing ceremony. The development of more formalized religion is reflected in the construction of earth mounds on which temples of wood and thatch probably once stood. Within a short time, ceremonial centers began to differentiate through the cooperative efforts of a number of farming communities. Pooling of manpower and economic resources permitted more elaborate ceremonies and ceremonial structures, but also promoted the breakdown of village self-sufficiency and encouraged economic interdependence and sociopolitical integration in the sustaining area. Rare and exotic raw materials were required to please the increasingly powerful gods, and their acquisition led to the development of trade relations between regions with different natural resources. Fine-grained, greenish stones were particularly coveted and beautifully carved and polished "jades" remained objects of special value in Mesoamerica until the Spanish Conquest. These kinds of innovations in settlement pattern and material culture are a tangible expression of significant changes in social organization, among them increasingly pronounced social stratification and occupational division of labor.

This Formative Period of Mesoamerican civilization reached its climax between 1500 and 1000 B.C. in the Olmec culture of the Vera-

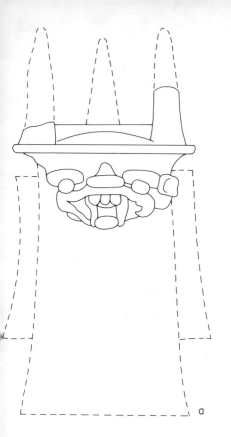

Fig. 19. The three-pronged incense burner is one of many traits indicating prehistoric communication between Mesoamerica (a) and the north coast of Ecuador (b). Although the feline is an ancient and popular ritual element in Mesoamerica and most of the Andean Area, it appears in Ecuador only in coastal regions strongly influenced by Mesoamerican contact.

Fig. 20. Grotesque faces with feline aspects are among the elements shared by Mesoamerica (a) and coastal Ecuador (b) and which imply prehistoric communication.

48

cruz coast (Fig. 21). Here, on islands in the swamps, dense vegetation has been torn away to reveal symmetrical arrangements of large ceremonial mounds, monumental stone carvings, and quantities of exquisitely worked jadeite amulets, celts, beads, and earplugs. Elements of Olmec art and religion spread throughout the central Mexican highlands and as far south as the Guatemalan coast during succeeding centuries, exercising so strong an influence that the Olmec have been characterized as the "mother civilization" of Mesoamerica.

Unfortunately, little is known of the sociopolitical organization and settlement pattern that developed and sustained the ceremonial centers. The existence at La Venta of earth platforms as large as 120 by 70 meters at the base and 32 meters high, arranged in a systematic plan around plazas (Fig. 22), implies the availability of a large labor force and of planners and supervisors to direct it. The highly formalized and exquisitely executed art style attests to the existence of trained craftsmen, while transportation of stones weighing up to 50 tons for more than 100 kilometers indicates mechanical and engineering knowledge of some sophistication. The significance of the giant basalt human heads (Fig. 23) is unknown, but Olmec religious art in general revolves around the were-jaguar, which combines feline and infantile human aspects and is believed to represent a rain god (Fig. 24). The drooping mouth is a hallmark of Olmec art, along with elegant simplicity.

The collapse of the ceremonial centers in the last centuries before the Christian era is as mysterious as their origin. One might speculate, however, that the conservative tendencies of a highly structured religion may have prevented alterations necessary to cope with changing social or economic conditions. Although Classic remains occur on the Veracruz coast (Fig. 25), the most spectacular civilizations arose elsewhere in Mesoamerica.

Teotihuacán, on the northeast edge of the Valley of Mexico, was already a planned city covering some 7.6 square kilometers by around 300 B.C. By A.D. 600, it occupied 20 square kilometers and had a probable population of 125,000, making it one of the largest preindustrial cities in the world (Millon, 1970). The tremendous Pyramid of the Sun, 210 meters square at the base and 64 meters high, dominated the ceremonial sector (Fig. 26). Ceremonial platforms and plazas were

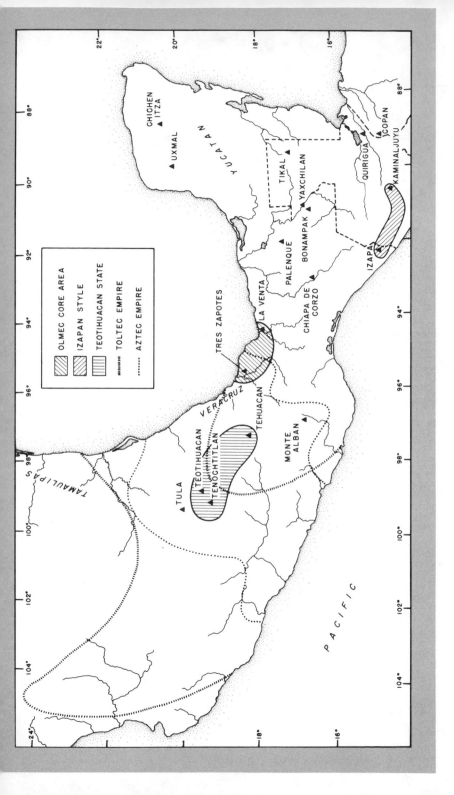

Fig. 21. Location of selected significant sites and the boundaries of
the principal prehistoric cultures and empires of Mesoamerica.

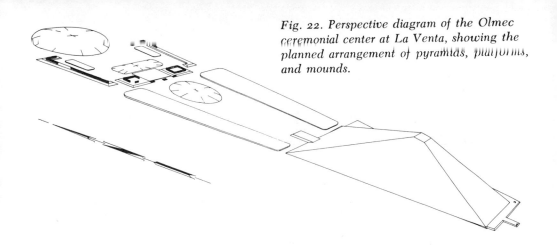

Fig. 22. Perspective diagram of the Olmec ceremonial center at La Venta, showing the planned arrangement of pyramids, platforms, and mounds.

Fig. 23. Olmec colossal head, one of many of similar size and style found in the Olmec heartland. This example, from La Venta, is 2.7 meters high.

Fig. 24. Olmec ceremonial ax carved from green serpentine. The shape of the mouth is a diagnostic feature of Olmec art. Although the jaguar was an important ingredient in the religion, depictions like this "were-jaguar" seldom show the protruding canines and prominent claws characteristic of feline renditions in Chavín and later art styles.

Fig. 25. The civilizations of the Classic Period on the Veracruz coast are still poorly known, but this carving on the slate back of a mirror typifies the distinctive art style of the region. Issuing from the mouth of the kneeling figure is a "speech scroll," a symbolic device that was elaborated in later times to the extent that the message could be understood by the viewer. Diameter is 12.5 cm.

surrounded by closely spaced rectangular dwellings, courtyards, storerooms, and other domestic and public structures of varying size (Fig. 27). Temples and palaces, built around courtyards, had porticos with square columns ornamented by bas-relief, and plastered inner walls decorated with brilliantly painted murals of prowling jaguars (Fig. 28) or deities with flamboyant costumes and scarlet fingernails. Between A.D. 300 and 600, Teotihuacán dominated central Mexico and exerted political, religious, commercial, and artistic influence as far south as Guatemala. Around A.D. 600, it was suddenly destroyed. The blame is put on the northern "barbarians," who, like the Germanic tribes that subdued Rome, succeeded in overwhelming their more civilized neighbors who were presumably made complacent by the security and comfort of settled life.

About the time that Teotihuacán began its elaboration, similar trends of increasing complexity under way in southern Mesoamerica reached their culmination in Maya civilization. The roots of the Maya are numerous and dispersed, and the origin of some of the most significant cultural elements is still unknown. It is now evident, however, that many developed outside what later became the Maya heartland. The earliest known inscriptions are on Stela 2 at Chiapa de Corzo in central Chiapas, dated December 9, 36 B.C., and on Stela C at the Olmec site of Tres Zapotes in Veracruz, with a date of 31 B.C. Many elements of Maya art are foreshadowed in the Izapan style, which flourished in southern Guatemala around the beginning of the Christian era (Fig. 21). Writing and the complicated Calendar Round were in use here several centuries prior to their appearance in the lowland Maya area. Earthen pyramids constructed at Kaminaljuyú near Guatemala City contain rich tombs, the contents of which reveal a high development of ceramics, stone carving, and more perishable arts. Around A.D. 300, the highland Guatemalan centers went into a decline. A century later, there was a brief revival, which architectural innovations and tomb contents indicate to have been stimulated by contacts with the distant city of Teotihuacán. This renaissance ended when Teotihuacán fell and cultural leadership passed to the now flourishing lowland Maya centers.

In contrast to Teotihuacán, which was a planned city, Classic Maya settlements continued the earlier Formative pattern in which a cere-

*Fig. 26. The ceremonial center of Teotihuacán, an avenue bordered
by platforms that were formerly surmounted by temples, each
dedicated to a different god. This view is from the summit of the
Pyramid of the Moon, which is slightly smaller than the Pyramid of
the Sun in the distance at the left.*

54

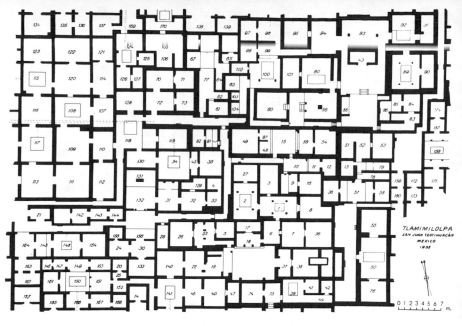

Fig. 27. *Detailed plan of part of the residential area of Teotihuacán. The planned, systematic arrangement of rooms, courtyards, and passages is typical of this ancient Mexican city.*

Fig. 28. *Portion of a fresco from Teotihuacán depicting a jaguar with a plumed headdress. Multicolored paintings of zoomorphic, mythological, or geometric composition preserved on the plastered interior walls of many buildings provide a fascinating glimpse of the artistic skill and imagination of the prehistoric inhabitants.*

monial center inhabited principally by members of the religious and social elite was supported by a farming population scattered over the surrounding countryside. Forms of social integration developed during preceding centuries supplied the labor for construction of some of the most magnificent monuments of antiquity. Maya ceremonial centers, which number in the hundreds, are irregular assemblages of platforms, plazas, pyramids, palaces, temples, ball courts, and causeways. Even as ruins, they are impressive not only because of the great bulk of earth and stone that went into their construction, but because of the exotic beauty of the mosaics, sculptures, and paintings that adorn their façades and interior walls (Figs. 29–33 and 35). Having learned to construct a corbelled arch, the Maya could top their pyramids with stone temples, whose massive appearance was relieved by a soaring super-structure known as a roof comb (Fig. 29). The six steep-sided Tikal pyramids are the loftiest Maya structures, the tallest rising 70 meters above the adjacent plaza. Looming high above the crown of the forest, they must have been an awesome spectacle, inspiring in the peasant population the same kind of reverence that was evoked in Medieval Europe by the great cathedrals. Like European cathedral towns, Maya centers were more than ritual settings and seats of administration; they were also places where farm products and manufactured goods were exchanged, along with news and gossip.

Details of the social organization that created and maintained the great ceremonial centers are still unclear, but the Maya penchant for decorating temple walls, stelae, wooden panels, and pottery vessels with an array of sculptured and painted scenes provides vivid glimpses of the luxury enjoyed by the upper class and of warfare and ceremonial activities (Figs. 33, 35, 38). The priests and rulers wore lofty head-dresses of long emerald-green quetzal feathers, ornately embellished clothing, intricately laced sandals, and heavy jade necklaces, armlets, pendants, and ear ornaments. They sat on thrones surrounded by re-tainers and rode on elaborate litters (Fig. 34) during processions along the elevated causeways that connected pyramids and palaces. In spite of this exalted status, however, their destinies, like those of their subjects, were controlled by the gods, and a vast store of astrological and astronomical lore integrated with complicated calendrical cycles was utilized to schedule activities and to ascertain the will of the gods.

Fig. 29. *Temple on the summit of a stepped Maya pyramid at Palenque. The scaffolding or "roof comb" supported elaborate decoration of a perishable construction, to judge from the depiction of a similar building on a decorative freize at Uxmal (insert).*

Fig. 30. Portion of a large quadrangle at Uxmal, constructed on a platform riddled with rooms and passages. Along each side of the plaza is a long narrow building bearing elaborate mosaic ornamentation on the upper half of the facade.

Fig. 31. Interior of a Maya building. The long, narrow, high-vaulted room is typical and results from the use of the corbelled arch in construction.

Fig. 32. The Castillo at Chichen Itzá, a symmetrical pyramid with staircases on all four sides. The serpent columns in the foreground flank the entrance to the Temple of the Warriors (see Fig. 41).

Fig. 33. Portion of a bas-relief on Stela 11 at Yaxchilán depicting subjects or captives kneeling before an elaborately costumed dignitary, whose face is concealed behind a mask representing a god. The quetzal-plume headdress, the ornate collar and belt, and the "manikin" scepter are typical accouterments of Maya rank and authority. The stela on which this carving appears is dated A.D. 756.

Fig. 34. Maya dignitary traveling by litter. He is accompanied by several attendants carrying burdens, only one of which is shown in this drawing taken from a painted vessel of the Late Classic Period.

Fig. 35. Painting on the wall of Bonampak Structure 1, Room 2, depicting warfare with spears. Most of the individuals in the upper left carry shields for protection. Elaborate headdresses are worn by many of the combatants. Bands of jaguar fur appear as neck, head, or ankle ornaments, while several warriors wear tunics of spotted skin and one (center) has a headdress in the form of a feline.

61

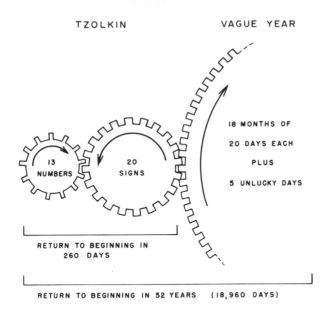

TZOLKIN   VAGUE YEAR

13 NUMBERS   20 SIGNS

18 MONTHS OF

20 DAYS EACH

PLUS

5 UNLUCKY DAYS

RETURN TO BEGINNING IN
260 DAYS

RETURN TO BEGINNING IN 52 YEARS   (18,960 DAYS)

Fig. 36. The Mesoamerican "Calendar Round" consisted of three intermeshing day cycles of different durations. The two shorter ones, known as the "tzolkin," completed their permutation in 260 days. It required 52 years, however, for the tzolkin cycle to run through all the possible combinations with the sequence of days composing the "vague year." The vague year terminated with 5 unlucky days, which were a time of apprehension since there was no certainty that another round would be initiated by the gods.

cu–tz(u)   tzu–l(u)   cu-ch(u)

turkey   dog   burden

Fig. 37. Translation of three Maya words according to Knorosov's interpretation of the glyphs.

Among noteworthy Maya accomplishments is a calendrical record extending from A.D. 292 to 889, preserved on stone stelae. The custom of erecting dated monuments not only provides a contemporary chronology unique in the New World, but furnishes detailed information on Maya methods of keeping track of time. The primary unit was a 52-year period known as the "Calendar Round," created by the intermeshing of three cycles containing unequal numbers of days (Fig. 36). The two shorter cycles, sometimes referred to as the *tzolkin,* required 260 days for the permutation of 13 numbers with 20 signs through all successive combinations. Simultaneously, a "vague year" of 365 days progressed through 18 months of 20 days each. The addition of 5 unlucky days at the end produced a close approximation to the 365-¼ day solar year. This system provided each Maya day with a double identification: (1) the number and sign of the *tzolkin* calendar and (2) the day and month of the solar calendar. It required 18,980 days, or 52 years, for the complete permutation of these two cycles, or the completion of the "Calendar Round." The termination of a 52-year period was a time of apprehension, since it was not considered inevitable that another cycle would begin. When it did, cooking fires were rekindled, monuments erected, and pyramids enlarged, accounting for the successive building stages encountered in the excavation of Maya ceremonial structures.

Keeping such close track of time would have been impossible without writing and mathematics. Numbers were written by combining two simple symbols (a bar, worth 5, and a dot, worth 1) with a vertical system of place values, increasing vigesimally (by multiples of 20) from bottom to top. There was also a symbol for zero, so that a number of any size could be written without difficulty, and addition and subtraction could be easily performed. To reduce the ambiguity of calendrical dates, special signs for periods of designated length were employed, and discovery of their significance has permitted us to read the calendrical portions of Maya inscriptions. The remaining texts have evaded decipherment until the past few years, when a new approach was suggested by the Russian epigrapher, Yuri Knorosov. He considers that the Maya glyphs represent syllables or sound combinations rather than letters, with ideograms added where necessary to remove ambiguity. Since many syllables are consonant-vowel combinations, and Maya words frequently end in a consonant, the reading of a glyph de-

Fig. 38. Scene on a lintel at Yaxchilán showing two priests, one of
which holds the head of a jaguar ornamented with quetzal feathers.
This carving is dated A.D. 726.

64

pends upon its position in a word (Fig. 37). The problem of decipherment is further complicated by our incomplete knowledge of the language spoken by the Classic Maya. Enough progress has been made, however, to indicate that Maya inscriptions may before long give· up whatever secrets they possess.

Around A.D. 900, Tikal, Copán, Quiriguá, and other great Classic centers were abandoned, calendrical monuments ceased to be erected, and the population appears to have suffered a marked decline. Why this occurred is another of the mysteries of New World archeology and innumerable explanations have been proposed. Many, such as warfare, insurrection, social unrest, loss of confidence in the priests, and refusal to pay tribute to the temples, are more likely to be secondary than primary causes. All periods of social crisis are characterized by social unrest and rebellion, but these are merely symptoms of more fundamental cultural disorders. It is doubtful that the Maya were any more aware of the real forces at work or how to combat them than are the rulers of modern nations threatened by strikes, spiraling crime rates, and civil unrest. There is reason to suspect, however, that the problem was primarily ecological.

Among the remarkable aspects of Maya culture is its environmental context: it alone of the major civilizations of antiquity appears to have flowered in a lowland tropical forest. While impressive buildings were erected in other rain forested regions, notably Cambodia, they are all the handiwork of civilized immigrants. The Maya have consequently presented a problem to everyone who has attempted to isolate the underlying causes of cultural advancement.

As the archeology of Mesoamerica becomes better known, however, it seems less probable that the roots of Maya civilization lie in the tropical forest. The fact that calendrical inscriptions and other diagnostic elements were present at an earlier date in Chiapas and highland Guatemala suggests that Classic Maya culture of the tropical lowlands may have reached its maturity in an alien and ultimately unsuitable context. Just as a young tree transplanted into a new environment often thrives for several seasons and then suddenly wilts and dies for lack of some essential nutrient, Maya ceremonial centers flourished initially and then abruptly ceased to function. Intensive exploitation of inadequate subsistence resources, culminating in soil exhaustion and food

65

shortage, could have been the cause but evidence remains contradictory. Studies of soil fertility, agricultural yields, land use, and other factors relevant to long-term productivity have utilized small samples from restricted and not necessarily typical locations. Consequently, some findings have seemed to indicate that a dense population could have been sustained indefinitely, while others have showed that food shortage is a continuous threat even at the much lower density prevailing in the area today.

Another enigmatic aspect of Maya civilization is the presence of a number of cultural elements absent in the New World outside Mesoamerica but widespread in Asia. Among them are the concept of the zero, writing, sequences of days associated with animals, sophisticated religious concepts (among them the tree of life), many architectural details (such as temples on pyramids, the corbelled arch, colonnades, serpent balastrades, and caryatid supports), art motifs, and elements of mythology. Although the possibility of transpacific influence has been vehemently denied by most Mayanists, the evidence is as good or better than that used to postulate connections between the Valley of Mexico and highland Guatemala, or between Mesoamerica and the Andean Area. Furthermore, while independent invention is conceivable in the case of a tool in which form is limited by function, the probability of duplication in art motifs, diety attributes, insignia of rank, myths, and other arbitrary creations of imagination is infinitesimal. To suggest that certain Maya Classic achievements were stimulated by transpacific immigrants does not diminish their significance. It does, however, make them easier to reconcile with the outline of world history that is beginning to emerge.

While Maya civilization dominated eastern Mesoamerica, the Mexican highlands were occupied by a number of regional Classic cultures. The best known is Monte Albán in the valley of Oaxaca, where the ancestors of the modern Zapotecs ruled from an impressive hilltop capital and buried their dead in tombs ornamented with beautiful frescos and furnished with rich mortuary offerings, among them ornate pottery urns representing gods (Fig. 39).

The Classic Maya decline coincided with the emergence of the Toltec, whose capital was Tula, some 60 kilometers north of the Valley of Mexico. In traditional Mesoamerican fashion, this city was also com-

Fig. 39. Zapotec funerary urn depicting an ornately dressed deity who holds a staff in one hand and a trophy head in the other. Pottery vessels of this type are common in the tombs of Monte Albán and other Zapotec sites.

Fig. 40. *Stepped platform at Tula surmounted by stone columns that once formed part of a perishable structure; one row consists of giant figures of warriors. The columns along the base retain traces of plastered surfaces; they are believed to have supported a flat wooden roof. The structure faces a large plaza surrounded by unexcavated mounds that probably represent smaller temple platforms.*

Fig. 41. Temple of the Warriors at the Maya site of Chichen Itzá, constructed by the Toltec. The form of the platform substructure and the colonnade along the base closely resemble the principal ceremonial building at Tula.

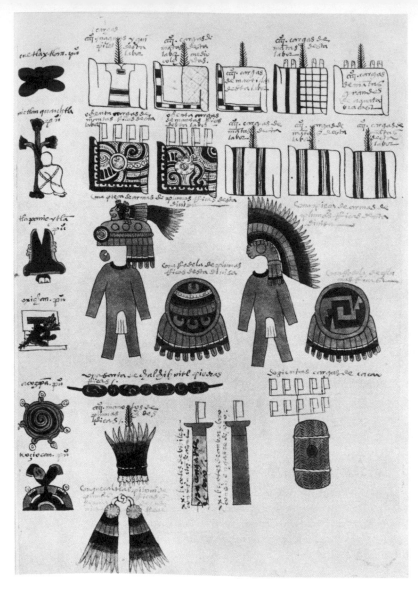

Fig. 42. A page from the Codex Mendoza listing the kind and number of articles each town was required to furnish to the Aztec Emperor each year as tribute. The towns are identified by the symbols in the vertical row at the left. The tribute includes cloth blankets of various patterns (top), ceremonial costumes with feather headdresses and shields, bundles of plumes, strings of beads, and sacks of cacao (lower right). Quantities are specified as follows: a thumb equals 1, a "flag" signifies 20, and a "tree" represents 400.

70

posed of a series of ceremonial plazas surrounded by platform mounds. A novel architectural feature was the roofing of buildings with wooden beams supported by stone columns (Fig. 40), some of which were giant representations of warriors equipped with atlatls, darts, and shields. Friezes with jaguar, coyote, eagle, and skull motifs decorated the walls. During its brief florescence, Tula exerted influence as far south as the Guatemala highlands. In Yucatán, Toltec conquerors injected new life into the fading Maya Post-Classic civilization. At Chichen Itzá, they erected a colonnaded temple more magnificent than the one at Tula (Fig. 41), and introduced the feathered serpent, the reclining human or "chacmool" altar, and numerous other religious elements and beliefs. After the destruction of Tula, about A.D. 1160, Chichen Itzá remained a center of Toltec influence. Shortly after A.D. 1200, however, it too was abandoned.

The last great Mesoamerican civilization was that of the Aztec, a primitive "barbarian" tribe that settled on the small islands of Lake Texcoco in the middle of the 14th century and grew in a few decades to dominate most of Mexico. This rapid rise is testimony to strategic skill and military organization, and it is not surprising that special military orders honored prowess in war during life and that Aztec warriors were elevated to a special heaven after death. Each newly conquered tribe was required to provide tribute to the capital of Tenochtitlán to support the growing requirements of the ruling class (Fig. 42), and the incorporation into the empire of regions with varying natural resources and of tribes with different cultural characteristics must have stimulated elaboration of the already ancient Mesoamerican system of trading and markets. Conquest was also the means of obtaining the large supply of human victims required for sacrifice to the powerful and insatiable Aztec gods.

The center of the Aztec empire was Tenochtitlán, a city of canals, plazas and markets, pyramids, temples, palaces, shops and residences, that began on an island in Lake Texcoco and swelled outward to the nearest shores, with which it was connected by causeways. At the time of the Spanish Conquest, it was a bustling metropolis of 200,000, so impressive that the Conquistador Bernal Diaz del Castillo was moved to remark that "those who had been at Rome and at Constantinople said, that for convenience, regularity, and population, they had never

Fig. 43. Reconstruction of part of the Aztec market devoted to the sale of fruits and vegetables. In the background is a building of the kind described by Bernal Diaz del Castillo, where grain and other articles were stored prior to sale.

seen the like" (1927, p. 178). The same author supplies a vivid description of the city as it appeared in 1519.

In this great city . . . the houses stood separate from each other, communicating only by small drawbridges, and by boats, and . . . they were built with terraced tops. We observed also the temples and adoratories of the adjacent cities, built in the form of towers and fortresses, and others on the causeway, all whitewashed, and wonderfully brilliant. The noise and bustle of the marketplace . . . could be heard almost a league off. . . . When we arrived there, we were astonished at the crowds of people, and the regularity which prevailed, as well as at the vast quantities of merchandise. . . . Each kind had its particular place, which was distinguished by a sign. The articles consisted of gold, silver, jewels, feathers, mantles, chocolate, skins dressed and undressed, sandals, and other manufactures of the roots and fibres of nequen, and great numbers of male and female slaves, some of whom were fastened by the neck, in collars, to long poles. The meat market was stocked with fowls, game, and dogs. Vegetables, fruits, articles of food ready dressed, salt, bread, honey, and sweet pastry made in various ways, were also sold there [Fig. 43]. Other places in the square were appointed to the sale of earthenware, wooden household furniture such as tables and benches, firewood, paper, sweet canes filled with tobacco mixed with liquid amber, copper axes and working tools, and wooden vessels highly painted. Numbers of women sold fish, and little loaves made of a certain mud which they find in the lake, and which resembles cheese. The makers of stone blades were busily employed shaping them out of the rough material, and the merchants who dealt in gold, had the metal in grains as it came from the mines, in transparent tubes, so they could be reckoned, and the gold was valued at so many mantles, or so many xiquipils of cocoa, according to the size of the quills. The entire square was inclosed in piazzas, under which great quantities of grain were stored, and where were also shops for various kinds of goods (1927, pp. 176–8).

The Spanish chroniclers reported Aztec society to be stratified, with the semidivine monarch at the top of the hierarchy, followed in descending order by nobles and high priests, commoners, serfs, and slaves, the latter being prisoners of war. The supernatural world was similarly structured. At the apex, the Rain God Tlaloc shared prominence with Huitzilopochtli, God of War, whose blood-spattered temple and altar (on which incense and three human hearts were constantly burning) horrified the Catholic Spaniards. Deer-skin books, or codices, recorded the deeds of heros of Aztec history, the details of rituals, the elaborate ceremonial calendar, and other kinds of information in a combination of pictures and symbols. Although most surviving examples are of post-Conquest date, they not only provide a great deal of data but also offer an insight into the Aztec self-image that is unique in the New World.

Social stratification, occupational division of labor, and a political structure headed by an absolute monarch coexisted in Aztec society with integrating mechanisms based on kinship, which were retained from their tribal past. Conflicts resulting from this transitional situation created an internal weakness, while heavy levies of tribute perpetuated animosities between the rulers and their conquered subjects. Powerful tribes such as the Tarascans, Mixtecs, and Tlaxcalans were never completely subdued, creating enclaves of latent disloyalty that made the empire vulnerable. The Spaniards were quick to recognize this situation and to capitalize upon it to bring about the Aztec downfall in the year A.D. 1519.

The Andean Area (Fig. 18, Area 1B). Settled life began on the Peruvian coast while subsistence was still based on wild foods, especially on the abundant resources of the sea. The aridity of the climate has preserved evidence of arts, crafts, and daily life not directly observable in most other parts of the New World at such an early period, including willow twig brooms, cactus combs, spindles with whorls of seeds, wooden bowls and trays, mats and baskets, fishline and other types of cord, slings, bags, belts, nets, and twined fabrics of wild reed or cactus fibers, some with fringes and tassels, others ornamented with openwork or transported warp or weft patterns. Semisubterranean, stone-walled houses provided shelter at night, and tangible manifestations of developing ceremonialism appear in the form of platform mounds. In the highlands, settled life lagged behind until plant domestication was sufficiently advanced to provide some degree of subsistence security. Between 2000 and 1000 B.C., however, the highlanders were living in stone-walled houses, building temples, and manufacturing pottery on a scale similar to that on the coast. Although the general level of cultural development was comparable to that in contemporary Mesoamerica, the specific content was different.

On the coast of Ecuador, by contrast, many features of the Chorrera culture imply a strong Mesoamerican influence around 1500 B.C. Highly

74

polished, thin-walled pottery with unusual kinds of painted decoration and distinctive vessel shapes appears at this time; delicate ceramic "napkin-ring" ear spools and thin obsidian blades are other innovations. Equally striking is the change in settlement pattern. Earlier pottery-making groups concentrated near the shore, where they could exploit the resources of the sea, but Chorrera sites also occur along the rivers of the Guayas basin (Fig. 44). This inland expansion indicates a significant increase in agricultural productivity, which provided the foundation for greater sociopolitical complexity.

About 1000 B.C., a remarkable and influential religious center emerged at Chavín de Huántar in the north Peruvian highlands. The site consists of a group of stone-faced platforms arranged around a plaza. Inside the principal structure is a complicated network of narrow passages and blind galleries walled with stone blocks and roofed with slabs. The floors of some are littered with marine shells, bones of llama, guinea pig, and fish, and fragments of magnificent pottery vessels, which have been interpreted as offerings. The most spectacular aspect of Chavín culture is its art style, which features ornate and highly stylized felines, serpents, and raptorial birds (Figs. 45 and 46).

Although resemblances between Chavín and Olmec religious symbolism have caused speculation about possible Mesoamerican influence, local antecedents also played a very strong role. By 1000 B.C., subsistence resources were secure enough to support settled life on a scale that not only permitted but probably required the elaboration of ceremonialism and social stratification. Agriculture is vulnerable to unpredictable variations in weather and other natural hazards, and before the acquisition of scientific understanding these were believed to be under supernatural control. Increased dependence on cultivated plants consequently led to increased efforts to influence the gods. Religious elements introduced from elsewhere were often integrated into locally developing traditions, becoming modified in the process. Because of such transformations, the archeologist sometimes finds it difficult to distinguish between diffusion and parallel development, and in the Chavín-Olmec case too little is known of the antecedents of both complexes to pass final judgment on their relationship at the present time.

Between 1000 and 500 B.C., Chavín influence permeated most of the Central Andes, acting as a catalyst to local development. Although its

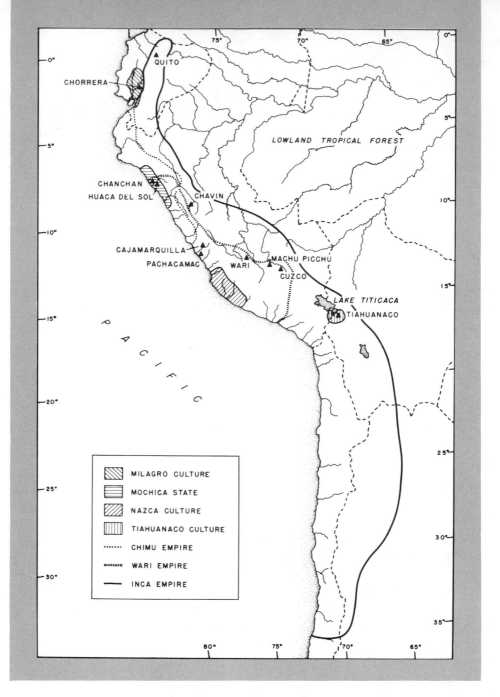

Fig. 44. The Andean Area, showing some of the principal archeological
sites and the extent of selected kingdoms and empires.

Fig. 45. Bas-relief of a feline with anthropomorphic features from Chavín de Huántar. The simple carving and naturalistic posture are in marked contrast to the intricate and highly stylized character of much of Chavín art.

Fig. 46. Rolled-out drawing of the decoration carved on a column at Chavín de Huántar. The intricate intermingling of feline, avian, and reptilian elements is characteristic of the Chavín art style.

77

religious appeal must have been formidable, Chavín innovations included new food for the body as well as the soul. At this time, manioc and several Mesoamerican domesticates, including the avocado and a higher yielding variety of maize, were added to the roster of cultigens. Improved methods of cultivation may also have enhanced the productivity of agriculture. The consequence was an increase in the number of settlements, an elaboration of ceremonial construction, and a proliferation of luxury goods in the form of jet mirrors, finger rings, ornamental stone sculpture, and pottery vessels, often with feline motifs (Fig. 47).

When the Christian era began, multi-valley states or kingdoms were beginning to emerge both on the coast and in the highlands. Approximately contemporary with the Mesoamerican Classic, the Andean Regional Developmental or Florescent Period was characterized by distinctive and exquisite creations in pottery, textiles, stone, wood, and metal. Particularly outstanding is the art associated with the Tiahuanaco, Nazca, and Mochica cultures. Of these, the Mochica is the best known because the information from archeological investigations is supplemented by an extraordinary pictorial record provided by a vast output of painted and modeled pottery. Flora and fauna of economic or religious significance (16 kinds of fish, 35 kinds of birds, 16 kinds of animals) were reproduced with such realism that species can be identified (Fig. 48). Other myriad details of domestic and ceremonial life, fishing and hunting, warfare, dress, architecture, music and dance, insignia of rank, birth and death, and even the disfigurements of disease, accident, or intentional mutilation, are realistically depicted on hundreds of thousands of pottery vessels. This marvelous documentation reveals that many practices in existence at the time of the Conquest were already present, among them litters to transport individuals of rank (Fig. 49), runners to carry messages, and military organization. Also recorded are "barbarous" customs later abandoned, such as the taking of head trophies in warfare, prevalent throughout the Andes at this time (Figs. 50 and 51).

The Mochica culture developed in the northern coastal Peruvian valleys of Chicama and Moche, and at its peak was a multi-valley state exerting influences as far south as Casma (Fig. 44). Sites composed of thousands of rooms or houses attest to the urbanization of life, although

Fig. 47. Pottery jar in the form of a feline holding a human figure. This vessel is from the Gallinazo culture, which intervened between Chavín and Mochica on the north Peruvian coast.

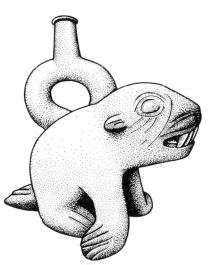

Fig. 48. Mochica stirrup-spouted vessel modeled in the form of a seal cub, a typical example of the skill in realistic depiction of flora and fauna.

Fig. 49. A Mochica dignitary traveling on a litter. Scenes like this
one, painted or modeled on pottery vessels, provide abundant
information on almost every aspect of Mochica life.

Fig. 50. Mochica mold-made jar showing
an individual with human attributes, except
for the prominent feline-like canines,
holding a trophy head.

Fig. 51. Portion of a painted cotton textile from Paracas on the south Peruvian coast, dating about the beginning of the Christian era. The man wears a jaguar costume and holds a human trophy head in his left hand.

Fig. 52. Partially excavated grave of a high ranking Mochica man. A covering of reeds, like those along the far side, has been removed exposing a variety of objects, including pottery vessels, baskets, feather ornaments, and three wooden staffs with beautifully carved heads. The gourds at the left protect the head of the individual.

planned arrangement is not yet evident. Large pyramids were erected for religious purposes and hilltop fortifications loom up from mountain spurs. The Huaca del Sol in Moche valley is the largest single construction in pre-Spanish Peru. Built entirely of mold-made adobe bricks, it consists of a huge platform 228 by 136 meters in basal dimensions and 18 meters high, with terraced sides and a causeway leading up to the north end. The pyramid on the southern summit is 103 meters square and 23 meters high. Also typical by this period are extensive irrigation canals, which brought under cultivation 40 percent more land area than is utilized today. Although we can only postulate the sociopolitical concomitants of such material remains in most other New World areas prior to the arrival of Europeans, Mochica vessels show us rulers and slaves, warriors and captives, priests and deities, artisans, and fishermen. Elaborate headdresses, woven garments, gold ornaments, carved staffs, mirrors inlaid with shell and turquoise, and numerous other objects found in excavations (Fig. 52) can be observed in use. We therefore know that the society was highly stratified and that the dispersal of Mochica art and architecture was a by-product of military conquest and political consolidation.

In the highlands, meanwhile, similar developments were taking place. By A.D. 600, the Tiahuanaco culture was at its peak in the Titicaca Basin, at an elevation of 4000 meters. Here, above the tree line, subsistence was based on the cultivation of potatoes, hunting, and fishing in the lake. The principal site, 21 kilometers south of Lake Titicaca, became a renowned religious sanctuary, attracting worshippers from distant areas. Platforms and sunken courts were constructed using stone blocks weighing 100 tons, transported from quarries at least 5 kilometers away, to be trimmed and fitted into walls with a precision not exceeded by the more famous Inca masons of later times. Joints were strengthened by copper cramps, and lintels were ornamented with bas-relief. Here, as on the coast, metallurgy was well developed. Gold and silver plaques, masks, cups, and other luxury items were reserved for the use of the upper class, but copper and bronze knives and axes may have had wider circulation. Tiahuanaco pottery was painted in black and white on a well-polished red surface with geometric patterns incorporating highly conventionalized pumas, condors, and serpents, as well as anthropomorphic figures (Fig. 53). The rigidity and angularity of these motifs are typical of Tiahuanaco art, whether the medium was pottery, stone, wood or cloth.

Another regional culture developed in the Ayacucho basin a little to the northeast. Its capital at Wari grew to be a large city of rectangular stone-walled buildings interspersed with plazas, streets, and platforms. Among the novel features was a complicated system of subterranean canals for providing water. Wari was subjected to intensive foreign influence, first from the Nazca culture of the south coast and then from Tiahuanaco. Perhaps partly as a result of these cross-fertilizations, the population grew and began to extend its dominance over the surrounding area. About A.D. 800, Wari influence reached the coast, where it was expressed principally in the adoption of new religious concepts and paraphernalia, especially the distinctive style of Wari ceremonial pottery. Some 200 years later, however, gross modifications in settlement pattern, technology, and religion bear witness to the forceful implantation of economic, social, and ideological patterns on the conquered regions.

Fig. 53. Human figure from a vessel of Tiahuanaco style from the south Peruvian coast. The hair or headdress, composed of feline, avian, and human heads, is reminiscent of earlier Chavín hair treatment (see Fig. 45).

84

Throughout the area of Wari domination, which ultimately extended from Cuzco to the northern frontier of the Mochica Empire (Fig. 44), urbanization caused abandonment of scattered villages and ceremonial centers. Cajamarquilla (Fig. 54), Pachacamac, ChanChan, and other impressive cities founded at this time all follow a similar plan, consisting of large high-walled compounds filled with rectangular rooms and separated by narrow streets leading to plazas, temples, and other public buildings. Irrigation works were expanded (Fig. 55), domestic pottery was mass-produced using molds, tapestry became the most popular textile technique, and a profusion of delicately carved amulets and ornaments inlaid with turquoise, obsidian, shell, and wood testify to the skill of the artisans. Occupational specialization and social stratification advanced to the point that at least 50 percent of the town populations were involved in activities unrelated to subsistence.

About A.D. 1200, Wari was suddenly abandoned and the empire disintegrated. Perhaps the growing cities began to challenge the authority of the capital, finally destroying its power. Regionalism temporarily regained ascendancy, but the Wari unification had an enduring impact on Andean cultural development. By establishing a secular form of government, an urban pattern of settlement, military organization, an interregional system of communication, and a state religion, it laid a foundation for the emergence of the Inca Empire.

Of the many tribal groups, chiefdoms, and states that filled the void, the Chimú Empire is the most extensive and best known. Originating in the general area of earlier Mochica supremacy, it expanded southward as far as modern Lima (Fig. 44). The capital at ChanChan covered more than 18 square kilometers and had an estimated population of some 50,000. Adobe walls 9 meters high and 3 meters thick at the base defined 10 large sectors containing houses, pyramids, public buildings, streets, parks, cemeteries, and even garden plots and stone-lined reservoirs (Fig. 56). Bands of geometrical motifs and mythical creatures carved in clay ornamented the walls of the principal buildings. Chimú arts and crafts show the effects of mass production and occupational specialization. Although the pottery continues Mochica and Wari forms, it is typically lustrous black monochrome and both the vessel and its decoration are mold-made. The decline of pottery as an artistic medium reflects the emergence of metal objects as the principal sym-

Fig. 55. Irrigation ditches dating from the Wari-Chimú Period on the north Peruvian coast. Such patterns, preserved in the desert, indicate that areas uncultivated today were agriculturally productive in prehistoric times.

Fig. 54. Air view of the city of Cajamarquilla on the central Peruvian coast, which was a major commercial urban center during the Wari Empire. Adobe walls of rooms and compounds cover most of the area. The broad white lines are modern roads cutting across the ruins.

87

Fig. 56. Air view of one of several large compounds surrounded by high walls that occur in the Chimú city of ChanChan. All structures are of adobe. The grid arrangement of streets, buildings, and plazas is a diagnostic feature of cities initiated during the period of Wari expansion.

bols of status and wealth. The Chimú were the master goldworkers of ancient Peru, producing vessels, ornaments, and decorative items of marvelous beauty, ingenuity, and complexity. Clothing was another important measure of social difference, and textiles consequently also exhibit great artistry. The paucity of pictorial art makes the Chimú Empire less vivid than its Mochica predecessor, but the relatively slight impact of Inca culture on this portion of the Peruvian coast attests to its cultural solidarity, as well as to the efficiency of its governmental and military organization.

To the north, on the coast of Ecuador, similar expansionist tendencies can be discerned in the archeological remains of the late period. After about A.D. 500, regional cultures began to melt into larger territorial units roughly coinciding with major ecological zones. In contrast to the coast of Peru, where rivers descending from the highlands intersect at right angles with the shore to create a series of habitable areas of similar ecological composition, the Ecuadorian coast is divided between a littoral strip and an interior basin drained by a network of southward flowing rivers. During the late period, this geographical dichotomy led to the emergence of two distinct cultures, one adapted to the interior riverine environment and the other to the open sea. Ecuadorian coastal waters are among the world's best fishing grounds, and exploitation of this subsistence resource led to skill in navigation and ultimately to the pre-eminence of the Manteño in coastwise trade. Pizarro's first expedition southward from Panama in A.D. 1525 encountered a large raft off the northern Ecuadorian coast, which was loaded with produce including crowns, diadems, beads, bracelets and other metal ornaments, belts, armour and breastplates, small tweezers, bells, and a quantity of textiles of wool and cotton "intricately worked with rich colors of scarlet, crimson, blue and yellow and every other color, in a variety of techniques and figures of birds and animals and fish and small trees" (Sámanos, 1844, p. 197). Since the Manteño, like their Chimú neighbors to the south, did not leave a pictorial record on their ceramics and since the climate of the Ecuadorian coast is hostile to the preservation of objects of perishable materials, early Spanish accounts like this one provide valuable evidence that the late Ecuadorian cultures did not differ significantly in level of complexity from those of contemporary Peru.

The archeological record is more complete for the Milagro culture of the Guayas basin. The existence of hundreds of small house platforms and the construction of many massive earth mounds for ceremonial and burial purposes imply a considerable population, and differences in the quantity and quality of grave offerings reflect marked social stratification. Sophisticated metallurgical techniques were employed in the production of elegant gold and silver ornaments encrusted with turquoise beads (Fig. 57) and of a variety of copper objects, including axes, knives, chisels, tweezers, needles, and fishhooks. The few textile fragments that have survived show skill in the manipulation of the tie-dye technique equal to the best Peruvian achievements. A number of new traits appear to be of Mesoamerican origin, among them ornamental inlays in the front teeth and thin ax-shaped copper plates as a standard of value. Whether the Milagro culture represents an empire comparable to those to the south or a looser kind of sociopolitical integration is not known; it is a matter of record, however, that although the Inca subjugated the inhabitants of the highland basins, they were unsuccessful in their attempts to dominate the Ecuadorian coast.

The Inca, who developed one of the most remarkable political organizations that has yet graced this earth, began as humble highland farmers and llama herders. Prior to about A.D. 1438, their domain was a small area in the vicinity of Cuzco; by A.D. 1470, they ruled supreme from Quito to Lake Titicaca, and 25 years later their frontiers extended from southern Colombia to central Chile (Fig. 44). Control over an empire with a horizontal extension of some 5200 kilometers and an altitudinal variation of 4000 meters was maintained by systematic application of ingenious administrative measures, which incorporated several elements ancient in Andean culture. For example, the Inca relay runners, who could bring fresh fish from the seashore to the dining table of the Emperor in Cuzco in two days and transmit a message the length of the Empire in two weeks, are a refinement of the couriers depicted on Mochica pottery vessels. The famed Inca highways, with staircases and tunnels chiseled out of solid rock, suspension bridges crossing streams and gorges, and rest houses at regular intervals for official travelers, are foreshadowed by the less extensive road systems of Wari times. The closely fitted stone masonry that is the hallmark of Inca architecture (Figs. 58, 59 and 62) has its antecedents in Tiahuanaco

Fig. 57. Gold nose ornaments from the Milagro culture, which occupied the Guayas basin of coastal Ecuador during the late period. a, a single wire changing from diamond-shaped cross section at the center to circular in the undulating margin to a thicker diamond forming the hook; b, flat wire coils utilized as a foundation for S-shaped pieces of wire and flat rings, which frame inlaid turquoise disks; c, reverse of a complicated arrangement of flattened coils soldered together. The opposite side is covered with turquoise disks bordered by tiny gold balls.

Fig. 58. Ruins of Machu Picchu, a late Inca city in the mountains
north of Cuzco. Houses and other kinds of structures surround a plaza
on the summit of the ridge, while agricultural terraces extend down
the slopes until they become nearly vertical. On the higher peak in
the distance are several buildings and agricultural terraces, which
appear as faint horizontal lines just below the summit.

Fig. 59. Part of Machu Picchu, showing the manner in which natural outcrops were incorporated into the construction. The stairway at the lower left is cut from bedrock, in contrast to the one above it, which is made of shaped blocks. The circular building is erected on another natural outcrop.

stone construction. The litter in which the Emperor traveled and other accouterments of rank were prerogatives of earlier Mochica rulers (Fig. 49).

What apparently was new, and what made possible a stable political integration of such magnitude in the absence of communication more rapid than the human leg and more permanent than the human memory, was a set of astute administrative procedures that effectively eliminated the possibility of successful revolution. Details are provided by Garcilaso de la Vega, Cieza de León, and other chroniclers of the early historical period. After the voluntary surrender or forceful conquest of a new area, one or more of the following procedures was put into effect. Local chiefs were incorporated into the administrative bureaucracy at a rank determined by the number of their subjects. Some of their sons were taken to Cuzco to be educated with boys of the Inca nobility, a measure that permitted their cultural and political indoctrination while also guaranteeing the good behavior of their fathers. Local images and their attendant priests were also brought to Cuzco and formally incorporated into the state religious hierarchy. The official language, Quechua, and the state religion were made mandatory; the highway was extended and storehouses and other government buildings were constructed; local resources were appraised as a basis for levying tribute; and, if resistance was severe or prolonged, populations of whole villages were removed to distant parts of the Empire and replaced with loyal subjects familiar with the procedures and requirements of existence under Inca administration. This political superstructure, which made Inca culture unique, has left little mark on the archeological record. The translocation of populations sometimes is evident in the appearance of pottery vessels of typical Cuzco style in distant places, and remains of Inca roads and buildings occur throughout the former domain, but settlement pattern, tools and utensils, pottery vessel shapes and techniques of decoration generally continue ancient local traditions. A major factor in the success of Inca administration was an ability to recognize which local customs were a threat to political solidarity and which were harmless and could be allowed to persist, thus minimizing sources of dissatisfaction that might erupt into violence.

The Inca administrative system was simple in conception, and its complexity derives from the magnitude of the population to which it

94

was applied. Geographically, the Empire was divided into four quarters, each of which in turn was divided into successively smaller units, ideally containing 10,000, 5000, 1000, 500, 100, 50, and 10 heads of families. Other groupings were made on the basis of sex and age, each category having well defined duties and privileges. Trained accountants kept census records up to date, so that when labor was required for the army or for construction, mining or some other activity, the manpower available in each region was easily ascertained. Taxes were paid in produce or in labor, and when absence from home was required, support was provided from public warehouses. Records of tremendous volume and variety were kept without the use of writing. The only aid to memory was the quipu, a cord from which were suspended a series of strings with knots arranged so that their position and complexity could be translated into numbers. The product being counted, the storehouse or region represented, and other details had to be remembered, and specialists were charged with this task (Fig. 60).

Fig. 60. Lacking writing, the Inca kept accounts of the kinds and quantities of produce in storage, as well as of population, size of herds, and other information necessary for efficient administration with a device known as a quipu. The quipu recorded only numbers and specialists were trained to memorize, with the aid of color coding, the regions and kinds of materials tabulated. This late 16th century depiction of an accountant has simplified the quipu by omitting the knots, which were standardized in form and position on each pendant string.

95

Fig. 61. Inca agricultural terraces have completely remodeled this Peruvian highland basin, making all but the steepest rocky slopes usable for growing crops.

The vast quantities of provisions that supported the civil and religious hierarchies, the corvée labor, the professional artisans, and the armies were obtained by a form of taxation levied on the ayllu, a kin group that was the minimal administrative unit. The land holdings of each ayllu were divided into three parts, one for the Emperor, one for the gods, and one for the ayllu members. The amount of cultivable land was increased in the highlands by terracing (Fig. 61), and on the coast by expansion of irrigation. Produce collected in excess of immediate requirements was stored in warehouses throughout the Empire to be withdrawn in time of need, whether to supply the army or the corvée labor or to relieve famine caused by natural disaster. This official redistribution took the place of the trade and market system so highly developed in Mesoamerica.

The heart of the Empire was the capital at Cuzco, a cosmopolitan city with impressive public buildings, richly ornamented temples, and streets bustling with activity. Cieza de León provides a detailed description of its appearance 30 years after the Conquest, when the impact of Spanish domination was still insignificant:

There were large streets, except that they were narrow, and the houses made all of stone . . . skillfully joined [Fig. 62]. . . . The other houses were all of wood, thatch, or adobe. . . . In many parts of this city there were splendid buildings of the Lord-Incas where the heir to the throne held his festivities. There, too, was the imposing temple to the sun . . . which was among the richest in gold and silver to be found anywhere in the world. . . . This temple had a circumference of over four hundred feet [122 meters], and was all surrounded by a strong wall. The whole building was of fine quarried stone, all matched and joined, and some of the stones were very large and beautiful. No mortar of earth or lime was employed in it, only the pitch which they used in their buildings, and the stones are so well cut that there is no sign of cement or joinings in. In all Spain I have seen nothing that can compare with these walls. . . . It had many gates, and the gateways finely carved; halfway up the wall ran a stripe of gold two handspans wide and four fingers thick. The gateway and doors were covered with sheets of this metal. . . . There was a garden in which the earth was lumps of fine gold, and it was cunningly planted with stalks of corn that were of gold. . . . Aside from this, there were more than twenty sheep [llamas] of gold with their lambs, and the shepherds who guarded them, with their slings, and staffs, all of this metal. There were many tubs of gold and silver and emeralds, and goblets, pots, and every kind of vessel all of fine gold. . . . In a word, it was one of the richest temples in the whole world.

As this was the main and most important city of this kingdom, at certain times of the year the Indians of the provinces came there, some to construct buildings, others to clean the streets and districts, and anything else they were ordered. . . . And as this city was full of strange and foreign peoples, for there were Indians from Chile, Pasto, and Cañari, Chachapoyas, Huancas, Collas, and all the other tribes to be found in the provinces . . . , each of them was established in the place and district set aside for them by the governors of the city. They observed the customs of their own people and dressed after the fashion of their own land, so that if there were a hundred thousand men, they could be easily recognized by the insignia they wore about their heads (1959, pp. 144–8).

Although the Inca practiced human sacrifice on some occasions, sacrifices of llamas, guinea pigs or maize beer (chicha) were more common. The use of a lunar calendar divided the year into 12 months, each of which had its festival celebrated with processions, dances, and offerings. Viracocha, the creator, was the chief deity, but the Sun, which was associated with the ruling family, appears to have been accorded more prominence than other secondary deities representing heavenly bodies. Great temples were dedicated to these gods, and served by priests. Young girls selected for their beauty resided in adjacent nunneries, where they toiled to create elaborate textiles for the glory of the gods and the use of the divine ruler.

The Inca sociopolitical organization, marvelously adapted to the administration of the Empire, was unable to cope with the unexpected intrusion of men from a totally different world—that of 16th century Spain. The Spaniards arrived at what was for them an opportune moment. In 1532, a civil war was in progress between Atahualpa and Huascar, half-brothers who disputed each other's claim to their father's throne. The Empire was thus more vulnerable than it otherwise would have been. Gold, silver, and precious jewels beyond their wildest imaginings brought out the worst in the Spanish soldiers, most of whom were of low class origin, and the resulting devastation was graphically described by Cieza, who wrote, "wherever the Spaniards have passed . . . it is as though a fire had gone, destroying everything in its path" (1959, p. 62). The Inca Empire, created in a few short decades, disap-

Fig. 62. The Callejón de Loreto in Cuzco; although the sidewalk and the upper parts of the buildings are recent, the lower walls are original and the general appearance of the Inca street is preserved.

peared within a lifetime, leaving splendid architectural ruins as enduring testimony to its brief glory.

THE INTERMEDIATE OR CIRCUM-CARIBBEAN AREA

Between the southern limits of Mesoamerica and the northern boundary of the Inca Empire, the land narrows like a double-ended funnel, pinched to its minimal width at the Isthmus of Panama. The mountains diminish in elevation, reducing the magnitude of altitudinal and climatic variation. Temperate and subtropical intermontane basins, a habitat congenial to the development of high civilization to the north and the south, are fewer and smaller. The lowland, with warm temperature and high rainfall, is clothed with luxuriant forest, bordered along the shore by mangrove swamp. The Venezuelan coast is dryer and supports a xerophytic type of vegetation, but tropical forest reappears around the Orinoco delta and is characteristic of the string of islands that define the eastern and northern boundaries of the Caribbean Sea. Although terrestrial connections are interrupted in the Antilles, most islands are within sight of one another. The gaps isolating them from the mainland are also minor: western Cuba lies 195 kilometers off the Yucatán peninsula and Granada is only 145 kilometers north of Trinidad (Fig. 63). Migration and diffusion were also encouraged by the general environmental uniformity, which provided similar subsistence resources from both land and sea.

In spite of a relatively early transition from food gathering to food production and settled life, and in spite of geographical proximity and consequent accessibility to influences from both Nuclear Areas, the Intermediate or Circum-Caribbean Area (Fig. 18, Area 2) never exceeded the general level of cultural development attained in the Nuclear Areas before the beginning of the Christian era. Maritime communication between Mesoamerica and Ecuador, which effected the exchange of numerous cultural elements, apparently made no impact on the intervening coast. Influences that trickled across the terrestrial frontiers into Central America and Colombia and over the water to the Greater Antilles enriched local cultures, but failed to catalyze the development of significantly greater complexity.

Here, as in the Nuclear Areas, pottery making was introduced at an

100

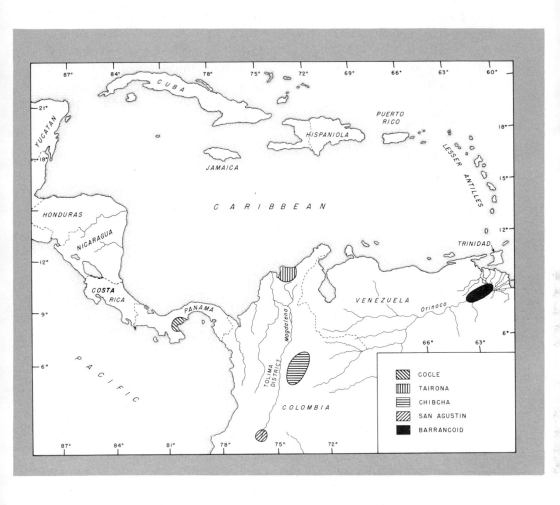

Fig. 63. The Intermediate or Circum-Caribbean Area, showing the location of a few of the prehistoric cultural complexes.

early time (Fig. 16). By the first millennium B.C., village life was established along the rivers and estuaries on the north Colombian coast, and there is indirect evidence to suggest that a significant fraction of the food supply was provided by cultivated plants. The presence of large flat pottery griddles, used by surviving Indians throughout the tropical forest for the preparation of bitter manioc, implies that this cultigen was already important. Fish, shellfish, turtles, and other aquatic fauna, which still abound in the rivers, estuaries, and lakes, as well as off-shore, were exploited, while wild plant gathering and hunting also contributed to the diet.

A similar adaptation was achieved by the Barrancoid culture, which appeared at the mouth of the Orinoco in eastern Venezuela about 1000 B.C. (Fig. 63). Many characteristics of the decorated pottery, among them broad-line incision, zoned polishing, filling of incised lines with red pigment, and zoned red slip, suggest derivation from the west, perhaps the Caribbean coast of Colombia. With the passage of time, these techniques give way to increasingly skillful modeling, and Classic Barrancoid vessels exhibit some of the most beautiful sculptured ornament of pre-Columbian America (Fig. 64). Although the culture appears to have flourished for several centuries, it remained restricted to the forested lowlands of the Orinoco delta and exerted little influence on adjacent regions.

By about 500 B.C., a number of distinctive local traditions had crystallized in western Venezuela, Colombia, and parts of Central America. One of the better known is San Agustín in the southern highlands of Colombia. Here, large earth mounds were erected over temples and tombs built of stone. Paintings in black, red, yellow, and white often adorn the walls and many contain sarcophagi and monolithic statues carved from basalt or andesite. The latter represent deities or persons of high status, and often have feline attributes (Fig. 65). The populace that erected these monuments lived among their fields in circular houses with thatched or mud-plastered walls. The abundance of metates and manos, which were used for grinding corn, indicates that agriculture was the primary basis of subsistence.

During subsequent centuries, a cultural dichotomy developed on the northern coast of South America in response to the environmental contrast between the tropical lowlands of the Orinoco and eastern coast

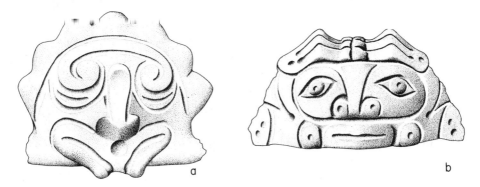

Fig. 64. Modeled ornamentation from pottery vessels of the Barrancoid culture at the mouth of the Orinoco.

Fig. 65. A stone figure from San Agustín in which feline characters, notably the prominent canine teeth, are incorporated into an anthropomorphic figure. A human trophy head is worn as an ornament. Height is 2.8 meters.

and the more temperate and mountainous western sector. In the east, the manioc-based subsistence pattern and plastic tradition of pottery decoration persisted, and as far as archeology can show, there was a high degree of cultural stability throughout the pre-Columbian period. In the west, by contrast, maize replaced manioc as the staple crop, and painting became the principal method of decorating pottery, although modeled adornos and effigy vessels remained popular. The population increased and arts and crafts were elaborated. In many parts of Central America, Colombia, and western Venezuela, stone carving, gold casting, and pottery making reached a high level of artistry (Fig. 66). Increasing differentiation in status and rank is indicated by the appearance of rich tombs, while the formalization of religious beliefs and practices is attested by the proliferation of ritual objects. Although stone constructions are rare, platforms, causeways, and other varieties of earthworks occur in many places.

The most conspicuous archeological remains are those of the Tairona, whose villages and towns occupied the lower slopes of the Sierra Nevada de Santa Marta in northeastern Colombia (Fig. 63). House platforms faced with rough or dressed masonry, stone house foundations, stone-faced earth mounds, causeways, stairs, stone-lined reservoirs, and drainage ditches occur interspersed with terraced fields. In addition to domestic pottery, vessels of complicated form with elaborately sculptured decoration were made for mortuary or ceremonial use. Figurines representing priests or warriors with animal headdresses, stone masks, polished stone beads, and pottery stamps are reminiscent of Mesoamerican products, while the highly developed metallurgy in copper and gold reflects Andean influence.

Although since fallen into ruin, Tairona structures were inhabited at the arrival of the first Spaniards, who reported that the largest towns had populations into the thousands. They also described occupational specialization in pottery making, metal working, stone carving, civil and religious leadership; extensive intervillage trading in agricultural products and manufactured goods, as well as intensive warfare and rivalry between civil, military, and priestly authorities. Villages sometimes formed temporary alliances for mutual defense, but the leadership of such confederations was transient and divided. This weakness ultimately brought about the destruction of Tairona culture, but only after

Fig. 66. Examples of polychrome painted pottery from the Coclé culture of Panama.

almost 100 years of intermittent rebellion against Spanish rule.

Mention should also be made of the Chibcha, who occupied the savannas of the east central Colombian highlands at the time of the Spanish Conquest, because they are often incorrectly equated in level of cultural development with the Inca, Maya, and Aztec. Unlike these three civilizations, whose achievements are richly documented in the archeological record, the Chibcha are known principally from early historical accounts. No ruins mark the location of their cities, and artifacts of stone, pottery, and metal are inferior in technique and artistry to those of neighboring groups (Figs. 67 and 68). The first European explorers found the area thickly populated and organized politically into autonomous chiefdoms. Boundaries fluctuated frequently, as conquered towns rebelled or were annexed to the domain of a stronger ruler. A Chibcha monarch held absolute power and was treated with great respect; no subject was permitted to look him in the face and no one was granted an audience unless he brought a gift. Chiefs traveled in litters embellished with gold, and sheets of gold often hung in the palace doorway.

What we know of Chibcha religion also comes largely from early Spanish accounts. Priests spent a dozen years in training and were required to fast and to observe sexual continence. Caves, mountains, and lakes, as well as temples, were holy places where gifts of food, cloth, gold, and emeralds were offered to the gods. Human beings, often children, were sacrificed to appease the Sun, to celebrate victory, to assure success in battle, and on numerous other occasions. The ceremony that especially stimulated the imaginations of the Spanish soldiers, however, was that practiced when a new chief assumed power. On such an occasion, the initiate was coated with resin and then dusted with powdered gold. Gleaming from head to foot, he was taken on a raft to the center of a sacred lake. While his subjects tossed offerings into the water from the shore, he submerged himself, washing off the gold, which settled to the bottom of the lake. The legend of El Dorado appears to have originated from this spectacular Chibcha rite. Repeated telling transformed El Dorado from a gilded man to a gilded city, hidden in the vast lowland tropical forest. The prospect of fantastic wealth has lured unknown numbers of adventurers to Amazonia and hope of its discovery survives in spite of centuries of fruitless search.

106

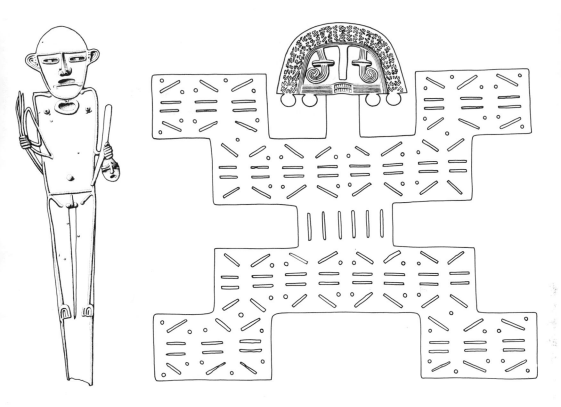

Fig. 67. Chibcha gold ornament in the form of a human figure holding a bow and arrows in one hand and a trophy head in the other.

Fig. 68. Gold ornament of the Tolima style from the Colombian highlands. The body of the figure is decorated with elongated and circular perforations.

Although the Antilles were colonized during the Transitional Period, pottery making and agricultural subsistence were not introduced until a few centuries before the Christian era. Diffusion was via the Lesser Antilles from Trinidad or western Venezuela. Pottery was not made on Puerto Rico until about A.D. 100, and the initial dates for eastern Cuba are some 800 years later. In spite of a slow start, the highest cultural developments in the West Indies were attained on Puerto Rico, Hispaniola, and eastern Cuba. Ceremonialism is particularly well documented by pottery figurines, exotic idols (zemis) of wood or stone, carved wooden stools, stone pectorals and amulets, and anthropomorphic pestles and celts, many of which have been found in caves used as shrines. Ball courts and stone belts worn by players of the ceremonial ball game are other characteristic traits. In general function, and sometimes in specific manner of execution, these find their closest resemblances in Yucatán, Central America, and western Venezuela, suggesting that communication took place across the intervening water. Since both the island dwellers and the inhabitants of the mainland coasts possessed large canoes, the absence of this kind of evidence of trans-Caribbean voyages would be more surprising than its presence.

Although they shared some of the customs and beliefs of the mainland population, there is no evidence that the inhabitants of the Antilles reached a level of sociopolitical organization comparable to that of the Chibcha or the Tairona. On the contrary, details provided by Columbus suggest that they were essentially village farmers. In a letter written February 15, 1493, he described the people he met along the northern coasts of Cuba and Hispaniola, who thus became the first New World residents to enter the pages of world history:

The people . . . , both men and women, go about naked as their mothers bore them, except that some of the women cover one part of themselves with a single leaf of grass or a cotton thing that they made for this purpose. . . .

They have no weapons, save sticks of cane cut when in seed, with a sharpened stick at the end, and they are afraid to use these. At times I sent two or three men ashore to some town to talk with the natives, and they would come out in great numbers, but as soon as they saw our men arrive, they would flee without a moment's delay. . . .

It is true that after they gain confidence and lose this fear, they are so unsuspicious and so generous with what they possess that no one who has not seen it would believe it. They give away whatever they may have, never refusing anything asked for. . . . This does not happen because they are ignorant; indeed they are of very subtle minds, and are men who navigate all those seas (Smith, 1962, pp. 185–7).

Within a few decades after this initial contact, the Indians of the Greater Antilles were nearly extinct, broken in health by forced labor in mines and on plantations, and decimated by European diseases. The focus of exploration and colonization moved westward to the mainland, where the material rewards were greater and the population was already conditioned to life in a society stratified into masters and serfs.

CHAPTER 4

ADAPTATION TO PERMISSIVE ENVIRONMENTS:

THE FORESTS, THE DESERTS,

AND THE PLAINS

Three distinct types of habitats occupy major portions of North and South America. Although the Forests, the Deserts, and the Plains differ in specific resources, they all provide a considerable variety of wild plant and animal foods and are suitable for intensive agriculture. In each pair of areas, the operation of equivalent adaptive pressures is reflected in the emergence of cultural configurations whose developmental history and general characteristics are remarkably similar.

The effectiveness with which the potentiality of each type of environment was exploited is related to the ease of communication with the Nuclear Areas, from which domesticated plants, religious concepts, and numerous other kinds of cultural features were derived. Proximity was less important than the absence of sharp ecological boundaries, but both factors played a significant role in hastening or retarding the acquisition of stimuli leading to cultural advance.

THE FORESTS

In North America, unbroken forest once covered the eastern United States and Canada, while in South America more than half the continent is still blanketed with trees. The hemisphere's two principal river systems are largely contained within these forest zones. In the north, the Mississippi absorbs the Ohio, the Missouri, the Arkansas, and numerous lesser tributaries as it flows southward to empty into the Gulf of Mexico. In the south, the Amazon is fed by rivers that rival the Mississippi in size, producing a discharge 12 times larger than that of its North American counterpart. Annual floods inundate low land and recede to leave shallow lakes stocked with stranded fish and marshes attractive to water birds. Large and small mammals inhabit the forests and edible wild plants provide a bountiful harvest in certain places and seasons. General ecological similarities channeled cultural development in the two Forest areas in similar directions by facilitating the adoption of some kinds of traits emanating from the Nuclear Areas and hindering the acceptance of others.

There are also important environmental differences between the Eastern Woodlands of North America and the South American Forest. In the north, the climate is temperate, with warm summers and cold winters, only southern Florida being reasonably safe from annual frost.

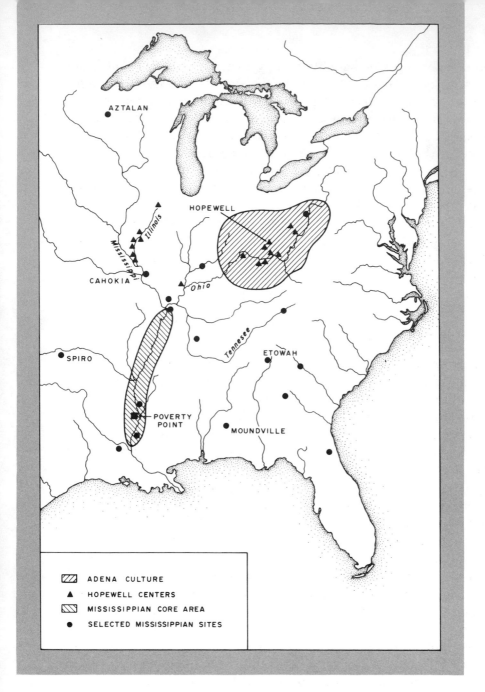

Fig. 69. *The North American Forest Area, or Eastern Woodlands, showing the location of selected sites and the distribution of some of the major archeological complexes.*

Soils are generally fertile, well drained, and productive without irrigation. The Mississippi watershed is separated from the eastern seaboard by the Appalachian mountain range, but this did not represent either a physical or an environmental barrier to population movement or cultural diffusion.

In South America, by contrast, the Forest lies within the tropics and only the far south is subject to occasional frost. Seasons are marked by differences in intensity of precipitation rather than changes in temperature and the vegetation is typically evergreen or semi-deciduous. Particularly in Amazonia, much land is permanently flooded; other large sectors are poorly drained; still others are badly leached. As in North America, the interior river basin is separated from the eastern coast by an upland region, but here it differs so sharply in climate, flora, and fauna that it constitutes a distinct environmental area (Fig. 18). As a consequence, cultural development in the coastal and interior parts of the South American Forest Area was largely independent.

The Eastern Woodlands (Fig. 18, Area 4A). Although pottery making was introduced to the Florida and Georgia coasts before 2000 B.C., and maize has been detected in the mid-Atlantic region prior to 1500 B.C., the Archaic hunting and gathering way of life appears to have been little affected. Around 1000 B.C., however, a significant transformation is implied by the rapid diffusion throughout most of the area of two new cultural elements: pottery with cord- or fabric-marked surfaces and mortuary mounds. The fact that the Poverty Point complex near the mouth of the Mississippi River, with an initial date of 1200 B.C., has large earthworks but lacks cord-marked pottery suggests that these two diagnostic Woodland traits are of independent derivation.

The type site of Poverty Point (Fig. 69), inhabited between 1200 and 400 B.C., has been termed the most spectacular aboriginal engineering achievement in North America. Dwellings occupied the summits of low artificial ridges that form six concentric octagons, the outermost of which is slightly more than a kilometer in diameter (Fig. 70). Gaps at the angles in the octagons provide access to the central plaza. Seven degrees south of due west from the center and immediately outside the living area, a large earth mound 23 meters high was constructed in the shape of a bird with outspread wings. A second mound, similar in shape and size but apparently not completed, is located two kilometers north

113

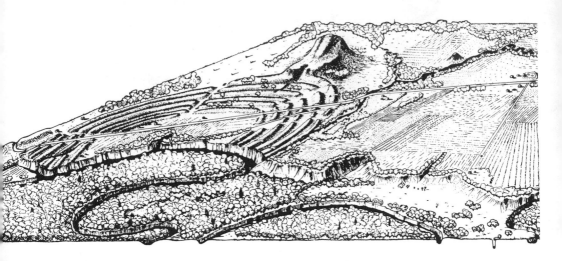

Fig. 70. Perspective sketch of Poverty Point, near the mouth of the
Mississippi River. The concentric rings are 1.2 to 1.8 meters high and
are broken by 4 aisles. Diameter of the outer ring is about 1200 meters.
The mound on the north edge of the rings is 21 meters in elevation.
A smaller mound is visible in the upper right. Vertical dimensions
have been exaggerated in the drawing.

of the octagon in a position about seven degrees west of true north. Stream erosion has destroyed the terrain east and south of the site, making it impossible to detect whether other bird effigy mounds once existed on these two sides as well. Mesoamerican influence is reflected not only in the compass orientation of the site, but also in the presence of petaloid greenstone celts, nude female clay figurines, stone blades struck from prepared cores, and small beads, buttons, and bird-head pendants fashioned from hard stone, all of which have prototypes on the Gulf coast of Mexico.

By 1000 B.C., small earth mounds were being constructed in the upper Mississippi Valley over cremation burials, a practice also observed at Poverty Point. These mounds contain deep, conical-based pottery jars with cord- or textile-marked surfaces, distinct both in vessel shape and in decoration from the earlier pottery of the Georgia and Florida coasts. The general resemblance between this Woodland ceramic tradition and Neolithic pottery from northern Asia and Europe makes diffusion from the Old World the best explanation for its origin. Subsequent ceramic development in the Eastern Woodlands is a complicated and variable interplay between these paddle-stamped and cord-marked wares of northern derivation and the plain, rocker-stamped, incised, zoned-punctuated, and painted ceramic tradition of Mesoamerican inspiration.

Although the impetus may have come from Mesoamerica, the first important cultural climax occurred in the Ohio Valley rather than at the mouth of the Mississippi. The Adena culture (Fig. 69), which flourished between about 800 B.C. and A.D 200, reiterated the Olmec-Chavín type of social and settlement pattern, in which a number of small scattered hamlets collaborated in the construction of impressive ceremonial structures, in this case earthworks. Those in the form of rings up to 100 meters in diameter are presumed to have had ritual significance. The largest, however, enclose a log tomb in which one to three adults were interred. The grave offerings reveal the sophistication of Adena craftsmanship and art: gorgets, tubular pipes, and incised tablets of polished stone; beads and combs of bone or antler; bracelets, rings, pendants, and beads of hammered copper; spoons and beads of marine conch. Pottery vessels are simple in shape and generally undecorated, reflecting their domestic function.

About 300 B.C., the Hopewell culture was emerging along the Illinois River (Fig. 69). Expansion eastward to the Adena heartland led to a cultural climax in southern Ohio, and in subsequent centuries influences from these two centers extended over most of the eastern United States. In many respects, Hopewell is an elaboration of Adena culture. Larger and more complicated earthworks were constructed; embankments up to 5 meters high enclosed circular, rectangular or octagonal areas or extended in nearly parallel lines as though defining avenues (Fig. 71). Although some of the structures are on hilltops, the existence of multiple breaks in the walls makes a defensive function seem unlikely. Most of the geometric earthworks are associated with burial mounds of conical or elongated form. The largest burial mound at the Hopewell site measures 152 meters long, 55 meters wide, and 10 meters high. Incomplete excavation disclosed three offertory caches and more than 150 burials, some with rich grave goods. Other mounds contain multi-room log tombs with interments, cremations, and large quantities of specially manufactured mortuary goods, including chert and obsidian blades, freshwater pearls, engraved human and animal bones, and stone effigy pipes; thin mica or copper sheets cut in the outline of serpents, animal claws, human beings, swastikas or other geometric figures; earspools, panpipes, and mask or headdress components of beaten copper; polished stone atlatl (spearthrower) weights and textiles with painted designs. While most of the pottery continues the earlier Woodland tradition, a small amount was decorated with intricate zoned patterns.

Hopewell sociopolitical organization is poorly understood, but the richness and variety of the grave offerings imply the existence of marked status differences, as well as craft specialization. The presence of obsidian and grizzly bear teeth from the Rocky Mountains, alligator teeth and shells from the Atlantic coast and the Gulf of Mexico, copper from Minnesota, and mica from the Appalachian Mountains, attests to the existence of a far-flung trade network for the acquisition of exotic raw materials, which Hopewell craftsmen transformed into exquisite expressions of symbolic art destined for the tombs of people of high rank. In many respects, including the elaboration of religious art, an enthusiasm for foreign raw materials, and the construction of ceremonial centers where few people lived but many came to work, to trade, and to par-

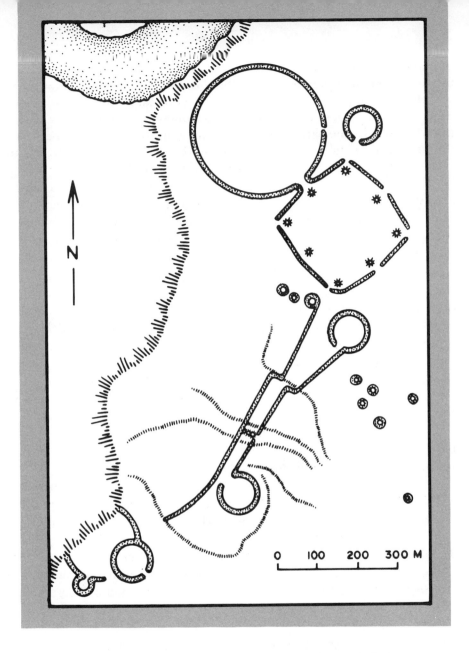

Fig. 71. The High Bank earthworks in Ross County, Ohio, typical of
the geometric constructions of the Hopewellian culture in the Eastern
Woodlands.

ticipate in rituals, Hopewell culture is reminiscent of Formative complexes in Nuclear America. As with the Olmec and Chavín cultures, whether the Hopewell remains represent political integration, religious unity, or merely interaction between autonomous communities is disputed. Also like the earlier Mesoamerican and Andean florescences, the decline of Hopewell was followed by a cultural climax in a different part of the region, in this case the lower valley of the Mississippi River.

Until recently, it was taken for granted that the level of cultural complexity indicated by Adena and especially Hopewell archeological remains implied a subsistence derived mainly from agriculture. It now seems, however, that primary dependence was on highly productive wild foods. In the lower Illinois Valley, Hopewell sites are concentrated on the margins of the floodplain (Fig. 72), at an elevation where they are safe from inundation. Five kinds of food predominate: (1) hickory nuts and acorns, obtained from the forested banks; (2) seeds of plants like marsh elder, smartweed, and lamb's quarter, which grow in dense stands on the mud flats left by receding water; (3) white-tail deer, hunted in the forest; (4) ducks and geese, which pause on the floodplain lakes during seasonal migration; and (5) fish stranded in ponds created as the river withdraws to its channel. Among tens of thousands of plant remains analyzed, only 5 seeds have been identified as cultivated squash (*Cucurbita pepo*) or gourd (*Lagenaria*). Maize has been encountered in other Adena and Hopewellian sites, but is so uncommon as to imply a minor subsistence role.

By the succeeding Mississippian period, however, subsistence was based on intensive cultivation of maize, beans, and squash. From a beginning about A.D. 700 in the lower Mississippi Valley, the platform mounds (Fig. 73), ceremonial art, and shell-tempered pottery characteristic of this culture diffused widely throughout the southeastern United States (Fig. 69), along with incipient urbanism and centralized political organization. While some hamlets contained no ceremonial structures, Mississippian ceremonial sites, unlike those of the preceding Adena-Hopewell, were typically also places of residence. Settlements ranged from villages with between two and eight mounds to cities like Cahokia near modern St. Louis, with 85 large mounds, more than a hundred smaller ones, and habitation refuse extending some 9.6 kilometers along the river bank. The largest platform mound at Cahokia

118

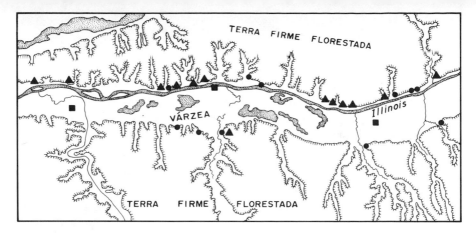

Fig. 72. *Early Hopewellian settlement pattern along the Illinois River. Except for a few summer camps (squares), all of the villages and mounds (triangles and circles) are located high enough on the slopes to escape flooding. Wild food resources on the floodplain, supplemented by hunting and gathering in the upland forest, were apparently sufficient to support a relatively advanced level of cultural development without significant emphasis on cultivated plants.*

Fig. 73. *Mound B at Etowah, Georgia, a typical temple mound of the Mississippian culture.*

measures 300 by 200 meters at the base by 30 meters high and had one or more perishable buildings of wattle-and-daub construction on the summit. Many features, including arrangement around a plaza, function as temple substructures, and construction in successive stages accompanied by the destruction of the buildings on the previous stage, reiterate earlier Mesoamerican practices. Numerous elements of pottery form and decoration, ceremonial art, religious symbolism, and social status (Fig. 74) also point to Mesoamerican inspiration. Without the foundation laid by the earlier Adena-Hopewell culture, however, the infusion of many of the new practices might have been more difficult.

Mississippian sites provide clear evidence of social stratification. The common people were buried in the village, accompanied by little or no grave goods, while individuals of high status were buried in mounds and provided with elaborate ceremonial and luxury objects. The manufacture of special items for mortuary use is best illustrated by the pottery. Throughout the domestic portion of a site, pottery is utilitarian in form and has plain, fabric-marked or incised surfaces. By contrast, ceramics recovered from burial mounds have a variety of exotic and biomorphic shapes, are often provided with spouts and pedestal or tripod supports, and are decorated by incision, punctation, or red and white, polycrome, or negative painting.

In addition to the type of luxury goods usually found with the dead of high rank, Mississippian burial mounds produce an array of finely made objects of shell, stone, pottery, and copper, decorated with a series of remarkable motifs reflecting the existence of a highly developed religious cult. In this category are shell gorgets, whole conch shells, and copper plaques carved or embossed with human figures dressed in elaborate costumes and carrying batons and trophy heads (Fig. 75). A considerable number of standardized elements, such as a weeping eye, a cross within a circle, a hand holding an eye in the palm, a human skull, and other more complicated and less easily described symbols, occur repeatedly. Other recurrent themes are the eagle, the serpent, and the feline (Fig. 76). Monolithic stone axes, chipped stone knives, and highly polished and decorated stone bowls are also characteristic accouterments of this religion, variously referred to as the "Southern Cult," the "Southeastern Ceremonial Complex," the "Buzzard Cult," or the "Dealth Cult."

120

Fig. 74. A wedding procession depicted by an early European visitor to Florida. The bride rides on a litter, seated on furs and shaded by a canopy. The litter, an ancient symbol of rank in Nuclear America (see Figs. 34 and 49), is one of the Mesoamerican elements introduced into the Eastern Woodlands.

Fig. 75. Engraved shell disk from a Mississippian mound in Tennessee. Mesoamerican influence is evident when the jewelry (necklace, bracelets, knee ornaments, circular earplugs) and posture of this figure are compared with carvings from coastal Veracruz (Fig. 25). The eye ornamentation, elaborate headdress, scepter, and head trophy are other typical elements of the "Southern Cult" in the southeastern United States. Diameter is 9.7 cm.

Fig. 76. Limestone pipe in the form of a feline from a Mississippian site in Alabama.

Fig. 77. Attack on a palisaded village in Florida, as depicted by a mid-16th century observer. Flaming arrows are being shot to set fire to the houses.

122

The only direct evidence of sociopolitical structure is provided by early French descriptions of practices surviving among tribes like the Natchez, who lived in nine villages along an eastern tributary of the lower Mississippi River in the 17th century. The Great Village, home of the high chief, surrounded a plaza flanked by two low platform mounds. One was occupied by the chief's house and the other by the temple. Natchez society was stratified into two principal classes, the nobility and the commoners; the nobility was further subdivided into three levels, each accorded well defined rights and privileges. The hereditary nobility claimed descent from the sun and the ruler bore the title, "Great Sun." The principal leaders in war and religion were close relatives of the Great Sun and their authority derived from this kinship. The ruler held the power of life and death over his subjects and at his own death was accompanied by wives and retainers to the afterworld. Others of his subjects sometimes volunteered themselves as companions, attracted by the prospect of an existence where "the weather is always fine; one is never hungry" and "men make no war . . . because they are no more than all one Nation" (Spencer and Jennings, 1965, pp. 418–9).

It has been suggested that the Mississippian radiation represents the dispersion of a population possessing an agricultural technology superior to that of the surrounding Woodland groups, who continued to depend heavily on wild foods. Mississippian sites from Wisconsin to Florida exhibit great uniformity in village pattern, pottery, burial practices, and other characteristics, and except in the region of development display no continuity with preceding local cultures. There is no evidence that this colonization was resisted by the previous occupants, who often adopted various Mississippian material culture traits. Leaving the Mississippians to the best agricultural land, they continued to follow their centuries-old way of life. Villages were small and frequently moved, as nearby fields were exhausted and hunting became unrewarding. Communal houses of poles covered with bark inhabited by an extended family were arranged in a circle, sometimes defended by a stockade (Fig. 77). There was little if any social stratification and division of labor was along sex lines. The first European settlers encountered communities of these Woodland peoples, whose adaptation to their environment was remarkably similar to that achieved in the hinterland and along the coast of the South American Forest.

123

The Tropical Forest (Fig. 18, Area 4B). Although it is reasonable to assume that Amazonia was inhabited by hunting and gathering groups as early as the surrounding region, the density of the vegetation, the use of perishable materials for tools and weapons, and the slight amount of archeological search combine to create a blank in the record prior to the introduction of pottery. The earliest ceramic complex, characterized by simple rounded bowl and jar forms, plain or twig-brushed surfaces, and zoned incised decoration, appeared before 980 B.C. on the island of Marajó at the mouth of the Amazon. Whether or not domesticated plants were also introduced at this time is uncertain, as is the route of diffusion. The presence of similar ceramic features on the north coast of Colombia several millennia earlier, however, suggests influence from that direction (Fig. 16). As was the case in eastern North America, this early introduction of pottery appears to have had little effect on the general cultural configuration. Sites are small and scattered, comparable in area and shallowness of refuse to Archaic sites of the Eastern Woodlands. The presence of tubular pipes of pottery suggests that tobacco may have been in use.

During succeeding centuries, small villages of pottery-making horticulturalists spread along the banks of the Amazon and Orinoco rivers and their major tributaries. Aside from simple, utilitarian pottery, sometimes decorated with incision, punctation or small modeled appendages, artifacts were predominantly of perishable materials that have not survived exposure to the tropical climate. The pattern of life must have resembled that of many present-day Amazonian Indians, who live in scattered autonomous villages, make simple pottery, and derive as much of their subsistence from fishing, hunting, and gathering as from the produce of their gardens.

About A.D. 500, a new ceramic tradition associated with a more advanced level of culture became widely distributed along the borders of the Amazon floodplain. Although many elements of this Polychrome tradition appear to be older in northwestern South America, not all authorities agree on a derivation from that region. Village sites are much larger than in earlier times, sometimes extending for a kilometer or more along the river bank. On the island of Marajó, where the best described remains occur, large artificial mounds were constructed for burial and, where it was necessary to create a land surface above flood level, also for habitation. One of the larger Marajoara cemetery mounds measures 250 meters long, 59 meters wide, and 6.4 meters high (Fig. 78). Several forms of burial were employed, some of which reflect differences in social status. The simplest are direct interments with no mortuary goods; the most elaborate are large painted urns (Fig. 79) flanked by undecorated ones, suggesting multiple interment to provide companions for an important individual in the next world. Small tools, tangas (pubic coverings), ear spools, spindle whorls, rattles, whistles, and figurines are among the ceramic objects found predominantly or exclusively in burial mounds.

Marajoara pottery shows a sharp dichotomy between domestic vessels with simple utilitarian forms and predominantly plain surfaces and mortuary vessels with varied shapes and elaborate decoration. One complicated decorative technique involves the application of two layers of fine clay or slip, first white and then red, and subsequent incising or excising through the red to expose the contrasting white surface; another consists of incision on a white-slipped surface followed by coating of the incisions with red. Intricate excised designs on red-slipped vessels often have the depressed zones retouched with white, heightening the visibility of the pattern. Low-relief snakes and lizards were sometimes incorporated, but modeling is typically anthropomorphic. Burial urns, stools, and ornate small vessels usually have a stylized human face on one side, often with weeping eyes. The most common technique of decoration was red and black painting on a white-slipped surface.

The subsistence base of communities bordering the Amazon floodplain can be reconstructed from early European descriptions. The first explorers were astounded by the quantity of food in all the villages they visited, particularly manioc, maize, and water turtles, which were kept alive by the hundreds in riverside pens. The floodplain lakes abounded with fish, which became increasingly easy to capture as the water level fell. Tremendous flocks of ducks and other birds came to browse on ripening grass seed, and in turn attracted numerous caymans (the Amazonian crocodillian). The water turtle, which grows to a meter in length, was exploited in all stages of its life cycle, including eggs, newly emerged turtles, and adults. The manatee, a large aquatic mammal, was prized for its meat. Among the principal wild plants were the *Victoria regia*, a giant water lily with edible roots and seeds,

Fig. 78. A burial mound of the Marajoara culture on Marajó Island in the mouth of the Amazon. The Rio Camutins in the foreground has risen during the rainy season, inundating the adjacent land. The family occupying the modern dwelling on the summit has cleared the trees for a manioc garden. The mound is approximately 250 meters long, 59 meters wide, and 6.4 meters high.

Fig. 79. A Marajoara anthropomorphic burial urn painted in red and black on a white-slipped surface. A large basin was inverted over the mouth as a lid. Identical faces occupy opposite sides of the neck; the only part of the body shown is a highly stylized arm and four-fingered hand. A circular ornament is visible in the ear lobe. The vessel is 83 cm. tall and has a maximum body diameter of 70 cm.

and rice, which grew in dense stands around the margins of shrinking lakes. These subsistence resources were available principally during low water, and the majority were too perishable to store for consumption during the wet season. Supplemented by domesticated maize and manioc, however, they could support a relatively dense population and a cultural configuration similar in settlement pattern and other aspects to the Adena-Hopewell florescence in the North American Forest (Fig. 80).

Shortly prior to European contact, a new ceramic tradition with antecedents in the Intermediate Area appeared along the lower Amazon. The most exuberant expression occurred in the vicinity of Santarem and the mouth of the Rio Tapajós, on the right bank of the Amazon, where anthropomorphic and zoomorphic adornos were lavishly applied to vessels of unusual shape, creating a rococo effect. Other indications of ceremonialism take the form of polished greenstone amulets, many representing frogs, and small pottery figurines of highly stylized execution. European visitors around the middle of the 17th century reported that idols were kept in temples and petitioned with offerings of maize. The chroniclers also speak of bustling towns of 500 or more families, where brisk trading took place in ducks, hammocks, fish, flour, and fruit. The Tapajós Indians were feared by their neighbors because of the deadliness of the poison that tipped their arrows. This capacity for self-defense also led them to be avoided by Europeans until more accessible sources of slaves were no longer profitable, but before the end of the 17th century their culture too had become extinct.

In the vast Amazonian hinterland, including the banks of most tributaries, a much simpler way of life prevailed. Little archeological investigation has been undertaken, but what information exists indicates that prehistoric pottery-making groups were similar in settlement pattern, material culture, social organization, and other respects to surviving unacculturated tribes. Habitation sites are restricted in area and depth of refuse accumulation, implying small villages with low permanency. Pottery bowls and jars were made for cooking, eating, and drinking, and seldom decorated. Often, there are fragments of large flat griddles on which bitter manioc was baked into thin circular wafers. Figurines, pipes, and other kinds of stone and pottery objects characteristic of sites along the floodplain do not occur. Ethnographic informa-

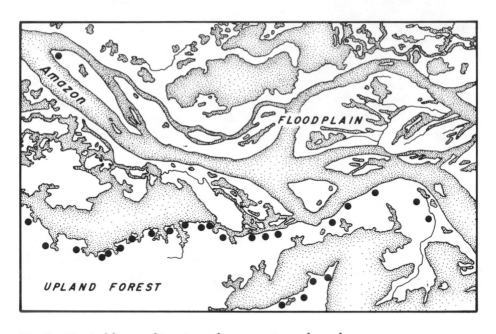

Fig. 80. Typical late prehistoric settlement pattern along the
Amazonian floodplain. The black dots, which represent habitation
sites, occupy high land along the margin of the inundated area. The
river and the innumerable ponds, lakes, and small connecting channels
abound in fish, turtles, and manatees. As the water level drops, it
annually deposits a new layer of fertile silt, making permanent
agriculture possible. The newly drained land also supports large stands
of wild seed crops, including rice. The region shown here is just west
of the mouth of the Rio Tapajós.

tion indicates that relatively low population density and high community mobility are related to a subsistence pattern in which wild plant and animal foods are as important as manioc, sweet potatoes, and other cultigens. As in less fertile parts of the Eastern Woodlands of North America, successful adaptation to wild food resources provided greater long-range security than intensive dependence on cultivated plants.

In the coastal band of forest, isolated from Amazonia by an intervening semiarid upland that impeded cultural diffusion, pottery making and presumably agriculture were not adopted until around the beginning of the Christian era. Initially, these innovations had relatively little effect on community size or settlement pattern. The presence of pottery in the upper levels of shell middens indicates that seafood continued to be exploited seasonally. Another wild resource that remained important in the diet was the nut of the *Araucaria* pine, and the upland plain of southern Brazil where this tree predominates is sprinkled with pithouses utilized as temporary residences during the harvest season. The pottery from these early sites consists of simple utilitarian bowls and jars with plain surfaces, except in the far south where fingernail marking, pinching, punctation, incision, and other plastic techniques of decoration were popular.

Around A.D. 500, a new ceramic complex appeared in the south, probably introduced by immigrants from the base of the Andes in Bolivia. This Tupiguaraní tradition is characterized by painted and corrugated surfaces and a multiplicity of vessel shapes, including large burial urns. By the time of European contact, its bearers had spread northward along the coast and then eastward to the margin of Amazonia, leaving enclaves in which the earlier population persisted. Interaction with the newcomers is attested not only by pottery of trade origin, but also in some cases by adoption of Tupiguaraní vessel shapes and decorative techniques.

Both archeological evidence and early historical accounts indicate that Tupiguaraní settlements consisted of several large communal houses, each sheltering a number of related families. Where warfare was intense, the village was surrounded by a stockade (Fig. 81). The shallowness of archeological refuse deposits indicates that villages were abandoned after a few years occupancy. The bones of the dead were placed in painted or corrugated urns and buried in or adjacent to the settlement. Characteristic stone artifacts include choppers, abraders, and large polished celts. The only surviving ornament is a cylindrical lip plug, often made from a greenish rock.

Although ethnohistorical accounts speak of multivillage chiefs with considerable prestige, their authority stemmed from personality and ability and carried with it little special privilege. The absence of social stratification is reflected archeologically in lack of differentiation in treatment of the dead. Typically, each village was economically and politically independent, and relations between villages were frequently hostile. Raids were made to acquire prisoners, who were eventually sacrificed and eaten. Taking a captive brought prestige to the captor, but imposed on the victim's relatives the obligation of blood revenge. This situation kept Tupiguaraní communities in a constant state of antagonism, which made European domination of the Brazilian coast easier than it might otherwise have been.

THE DESERTS

Regions of semiarid climate, moderate elevation, and xerophytic vegetation lie northwest of Mesoamerica and southeast of the Andean Area (Fig. 18). These Desert Areas are impressive examples of ecological convergence under exposure to similar climatic conditions. The mean **temperature at Tucson, Arizona is 20° C.; at Andalgala in Argentina, it is 18° C. Mean rainfall at the former station is 292 mm. per year; at** the latter, it is 272 mm. per year. The rainfall pattern is also almost identical, with precipitation concentrated during the summer. Although several of the dominant plants are closely related, most of the vegetation is composed of species with independent evolutionary histories that have converged morphologically to a remarkable degree. As a result, the Sonoran Desert landscape of North America and the Argentine Monte are extraordinarily similar in appearance.

The North American Desert contains three major and several minor ecological zones, which equate with distinctive varieties of Southwestern culture (Fig. 82). Southern New Mexico and southeastern Arizona, with forested slopes and grassy valleys above 2000 meters elevation, was the habitat of the Mogollon tradition. The "four corners" area, so named because the states of Arizona, New Mexico,

130

*Fig. 81. An attack on a palisaded village on the Brazilian coast, as depicted by a **16th** century European artist. The four communal houses probably each sheltered a number of related families. Trophy skulls are displayed on posts in the rear.*

131

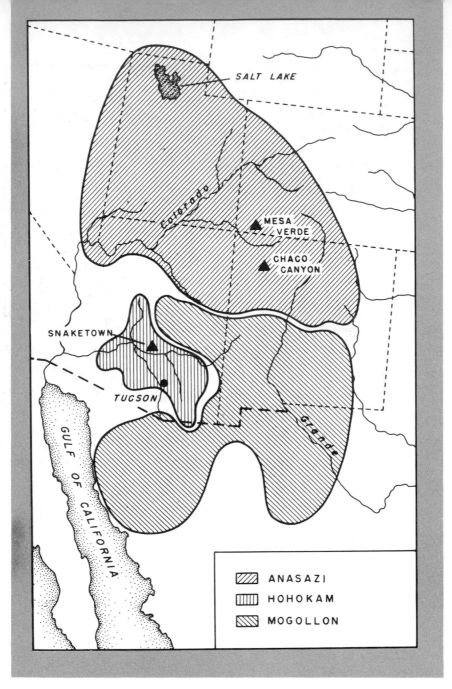

Fig. 82. Geographical distribution of the three principal cultural traditions of the North American Desert Area at the time of their maximum expansion, around A.D. 1000, and location of a few major archeological sites.

Utah, and Colorado intersect there and characterized by high plateaus riddled with deep canyons, was the homeland of the Anasazi. The low, hot desert of southern Arizona and New Mexico was occupied by the Hohokam. These "co-traditions" shared a common ancestry in the ancient desert culture of the Transitional Period and were subjected to influences of differing intensity from Mesoamerica and to a lesser extent from neighboring regions to the north and east. Although in many respects the Southwest can be considered a marginal expression of Mesoamerican culture, its history is not a simple recapitulation of events that took place to the south.

The South American Desert Area is also composed of several ecological zones (Fig. 87). The three principal ones are the Puna, a cold and dry region above 3500 meters elevation, the Valliserrana, composed of slopes and valleys between 1200 and 3000 meters, and the Sierras Centrales, with elevations generally below 2000 meters. Although numerous local complexes have been identified and regional variations are pronounced during certain periods, several major trends of cultural development and sources of innovations can be discerned. As was true in North America, the primary stimulus was from the Nuclear Area, in this case the Central Andes; similarly, the introduction of agriculture, pottery, and other increments of settled life was retarded by a broad zone of inhospitable terrain. Influences from the Forest were also pronounced, however, and communication with the Pacific Coast was more intimate than in the north.

The Southwestern United States (Fig. 18, Area 3A). While maize has been found in Southwestern sites dating before 3000 B.C., it had little subsistence impact and the traditional desert culture persisted with no signficant alteration until shortly before the Christian era. About 100 B.C., pottery with plain and red-slipped surfaces appears in the Mogollon and Hohokam areas, followed about 200 years later by red-on-buff painting. The typical design on the interior of hemispherical bowls consists of two solid intersecting bands dividing the field into quarters filled with concentric triangles, a type of decoration that was employed during the middle and late Formative Period in the Valley of Mexico. Recent archeological investigations in northern Mexico have begun to reveal a chain of simple agricultural complexes along the Sierra Madre Occidental, the probable route by which cultural influences passed from Mesoamerica into the Hohokam and Mogollon areas. Because the Anasazi occupied a more isolated position to the north, Mesoamerican influence on Anasazi culture was both reduced in intensity and retarded in time.

By A.D. 500, sedentary village life was well established in the Hohokam area. Farming the desert required irrigation, and canals 10 meters wide and 16 kilometers long were already in use by this time. Elements of art style and many kinds of luxury objects, such as turquoise mosaics, shell beads and gorgets, shell trumpets, and effigy vessels, have Mesoamerican prototypes; the most striking evidence of acculturation, however, takes the form of ceremonial earthworks. The ball court at Snaketown had a playing field 56 meters long and 19 meters wide, with earth embankments 6 meters high along both sides. Platform mounds were constructed in several stages in typical Meso-american fashion; the largest measures 29 by 22 meters at the base and 3 meters high and had a structure of perishable material on the summit. The climax of Hohokam construction came between A.D. 1200 and 1400, when multistoried "great houses" were erected, with mud walls up to 2 meters thick. Although the only objects of unquestionable trade origin are copper bells, cultural correspondences are so numerous and detailed that the process of diffusion seems inadequate to account for them. Among possible alternative explanations are: (1) the introduction of these new ideas by itinerant traders, who formed a special occupational group in later Mesoamerican society, or (2) immigration and coloniza-tion by Toltec nobility, who fled Tula at the time it was destroyed.

The Mogollon to the east, although participating in the early acquisition of ceramics, exhibit much less subsequent Mesoamerican influence than the Hohokam. An ecological factor may be involved, since the mountain habitat of the Mogollon offered less potential for intensive farming and consequently inadequate support for the elab-orate ceremonialism to which most of the Mesoamerican features in Hohokam culture are related. Shell bracelets and shell and turquoise beads were manufactured, however, and often buried with the dead. Here, as in the Anasazi area, the earliest villages were composed of 2 to 20 semisubterranean houses with timber-supported earth roofs. The maize harvest was stored inside or outside the house in pits. With the passage of time, Mogollon settlements increased in size and by

A.D. 950 they contained several units of surface rooms with stone and mud masonary walls. As is often the case with religious structures, pithouses continued to serve as ceremonial gathering places long after they were superseded as dwellings. Community leadership was exercised by a council, whose members were the heads of kinship groups. Each community was autonomous and social organization was essentially democratic.

The best known of the Southwestern co-traditions is the Anasazi, whose spectacular cliff dwellings and large "apartment house" ruins were the first to attract the attention of travelers and archeologists. As a consequence of initial scientific investigation in this area, where Mesoamerican influence was most diluted, pottery making and other basic cultural elements were at one time believed to have been invented by the Anasazi. This is one of the best historical examples of the manner in which the reconstruction of cultural development reflects the existing state of archeological information.

Anasazi culture has its roots in rock shelter habitations and small pithouse villages, which in the early centuries of the Christian era did not differ greatly from those of the Mogollon, except for the absence of pottery. By the Basket-maker II Period, between A.D. 400 and 700, the adoption of corrugated cooking vessels, black-on-white painting (Fig. 83), pitchers (Fig. 84), double-necked bottles, ladles, and other novel pottery forms, as well as the domesticated turkey and various other traits, signals the emergence of a distinct way of life. Between A.D. 700 and 900, paralleling the Mogollon trend, above-ground dwellings replace the earlier pithouses, which survive as ceremonial structures or "kivas." By Pueblo III, the Classic Period of Anasazi culture between A.D. 1100 and 1300, much of the populace was concentrated in towns. The largest is Pueblo Bonito in Chaco Canyon, New Mexico, a D-shaped complex of some 800 rooms, increasing from one story around the interior plaza to four stories along the curved rear wall. Its population has been estimated at around 1200. Numerous kivas up to 20 meters in diameter occupy the lower story. When the structures were in use, their flat roofs served as a plaza for domestic activities and their secluded interiors, reached by trap doors in the ceilings, were the locus of meetings and secret ceremonies conducted by religious fraternities. The size of cliff dwellings was limited by the dimensions of

Fig. 83. Motifs on painted pottery from the Southwestern United States.
The geometric patterns and stylized bird are from Anasazi vessels;
the lizard is a Hohokan motif. Resemblance to designs on pottery from
the Valliserrana region of northwestern Argentina (Fig. 90) is very close.

Fig. 84. Pottery pitchers from
the Desert regions of North
(a) and South America
(b). Although this vessel
form is typical in the Deserts,
it was rarely used elsewhere
in the New World.

a

b

136

the cavity, but the superposition of rooms to four or more stories permitted maximum use of air as well as ground space (Fig. 85). Cliff Palace, in Mesa Verde, contains more than 200 rooms and 23 kivas.

Population concentrations of this magnitude were made possible by refinements in agricultural technology. Check dams were built for conservation and control of rain water, and streams were diverted into irrigation canals up to 6.5 kilometers long. Although the construction and maintenance of irrigation systems of this magnitude have sometimes been assumed to require stratified sociopolitical organization, Anasazi leadership was invested in a council of elders. Differences in status and rank were minor, and the interests of the individual were subordinated to those of the community. Religious observances, such as masked dances and kiva ceremonies, were characterized by secrecy and anonymity, so that the emergence of social distinctions from this sector was effectively inhibited.

Pueblo III culture incorporated many Mesoamerican elements previously adopted in the Hohokam area, including copper bells, conch shell trumpets, turquoise mosaics, effigy vessels, circular towers, and parrots, which were kept for their feathers. The more flamboyant aspects of Anasazi ceremonialism, such as masked dances involving impersonation of supernatural beings known as kachinas (Fig. 86) and kiva murals featuring mythological scenes, made their appearance about A.D. 1300. After this date, many of the flourishing towns were abandoned and the Anasazi population concentration was displaced southward. Various explanations have been offered; drought-induced crop failure and the predation of nomadic hunting groups on the northern frontier are the best documented. About the same time, communication with Mesoamerica was broken off. The resulting isolation permitted development of the distinctive Pueblo culture encountered by the Spaniards, who first arrived in the Southwest in the 16th century.

Northwestern Argentina (Fig. 18, Area 3B). A few centuries before the Christian era, cultivated plants, pottery making and metallurgy appeared almost simultaneously in the South American Desert Area. In the Valliserrana region (Fig. 87), which is the best known archeologically, the initial pottery was plain or red slipped, as was the earliest Mogollon pottery in the United States Southwest. Decoration developed slightly later in the form of incised triangles, stepped elements, crosses,

Fig. 85. Cliff Palace, one of several large Anasazi cliff dwellings in the Mesa Verde National Park. The circular depressions are kivas, which formerly had a flat roof level with the surrounding surface. Walls behind are remnants of rooms, which are more completely preserved farther back in the rock shelter. Posts projecting through the wall of the square tower on the left mark the floors of four superimpose rooms.

Fig. 86. Doll representing a Hopi kachina or "messenger of the gods." Kachinas were also impersonated in masked dances that formed an important part of Anasazi ritual during the late prehistoric period.

and other geometric figures, which have prototypes in Formative ceramics of the Andean Area. About A.D. 300, polychrome painting was added. Typical settlements consist of two to five small, circular, stone-walled houses surrounding a patio; small pithouses also occasionally occur. Burial of adults was in the house or patio, and differences in grave goods imply incipient social distinctions. Cemeteries of up to 200 urns contain the remains of children. Terraced fields date from this period, as do ceremonial platforms and artificial mounds. Potatoes and quinoa were cultivated and llamas were probably domesticated. Sculpture in stone and wood was well developed, while an abundance of rings, bands, bells, tweezers, needles, axes, and other objects attests to the importance of metallurgy in copper, silver, and gold.

Between A.D. 700–1000, the Valliserrana region was dominated by the Aguada culture, whose florescent development in arts, crafts, and ceremonialism reflects Tiahuanaco influence. Bronze was introduced, maize was added to the subsistence inventory, agricultural techniques were intensified, and population density increased. Ceramics, decorated by incision or polychrome painting, reached an artistry never surpassed. Feline and "dragon" motifs on pottery, metal, and wooden objects may symbolize supernatural beings, while richly carved wooden tablets and bronze axes are artifacts of probable ceremonial significance (Fig. 88). Warfare was frequent, to judge from depictions of warriors and trophy heads (Fig. 89) and from the presence of decapitated burials. Social stratification is implied by variations in the type and amount of grave goods; urn burial of children was no longer characteristic.

The flourishing Aguada culture disappeared so suddenly and completely about A.D. 1000 as to suggest that an invasion was responsible, probably originating from the Forest Area to the east. Communal pithouses and black-on-white painted pottery were introduced (Fig. 90), urn burial of children again became popular, and bronze working was elaborated. During succeeding centuries, changes in settlement pattern parallel in a general way those in the United States Southwest: pithouses were replaced by small rectangular stone-walled surface structures, which increased in number and culminated in irregular agglutinations of 250 or more rooms. Typically erected on mesa tops, these towns bear a striking resemblance in material and method of construction, as well as in location and environmental setting, to ruins in the Anasazi

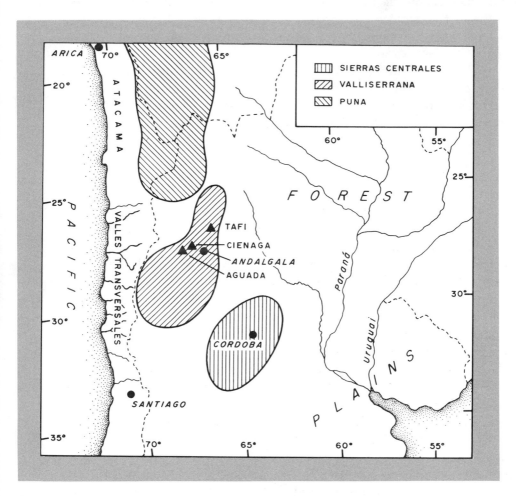

Fig. 87. Approximate location of the principal cultural subregions of the South American Desert Area and the adjacent Pacific Coast and selected archeological sites.

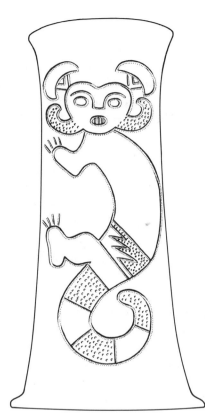

Fig. 88. Bronze ceremonial ax from the Valliserrana region of northwestern Argentina with a stylized feline depicted on one surface.

Fig. 89. Incised anthropomorphic figure from a pottery vessel of the Aguada culture, northwestern Argentina. Success in warfare is implied by the trophy head hanging from the right arm.

area. Fortresses also became common, implying an acceleration of warfare prior to the Inca conquest.

In the Sierras Centrales, to the south, the addition of agriculture and domesticated llamas to the earlier hunting and gathering subsistence pattern made less cultural impact. Quadrangular semi-subterranean houses were typical, and in later times between 10 and 40 were arranged in a circle inside a cactus fence. Rock shelters were made into dwellings by the construction of stone front walls. Common artifacts include grooved stone axes, bone and stone projectile points, bolas, mortars and pestles, and manos and metates. Pottery bowls and sloping necked jars are predominantly plain, but occasionally ornamented with incision, zoned punctation, net or basketry impressions. Direct interment of adults and urn burial of children follows the early practice in the Valliserrana region, and other aspects of the configuration prevailing in the Sierras Centrales up to Inca times are also reminiscent of the pre-Aguada pattern to the north.

Little archeological work has been done in the Puna and chronological differences there are consequently obscure. It appears, however, that this forbidding region supported a larger population during the aboriginal period than it does today. The vast plain, bleak as a lunar landscape, stretches northward at about 3500 meters elevation. Its surface is broken by a few low north-south ridges, and high mountains on the eastern and southern borders isolate it from the other Desert subregions. Light rain between December and February creates ephemeral streams that disappear into brackish lakes and extensive salt flats. Only protected locations, where altitude or drought were less extreme, were suitable for exploitation by communities dependent on the cultivation of maize, beans, quinoa, and potatoes, and on the herding of llamas. Agricultural land was extended by the construction of terraces, but irrigation could not be employed to supplement the scanty rainfall. Rectangular or circular stone-walled or adobe houses were constructed independently or in agglutinated assemblages, and stone-walled corrals were built to confine llamas. The dead were buried in caves, the crypts sealed off with a stone and mud wall.

Calabashes were the favored containers and pottery is uncommon and predominantly plain except in the late period, when black-on-red painting was introduced. Stone projectile points, mortars and pestles,

142

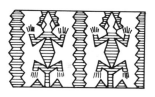

Fig. 90. Motifs on pottery from the Valliserrana region of the South American Desert Area. The geometric patterns, as well as the stylized treatment of birds and lizards, bear a striking resemblance to the decoration on pottery from the North American Desert (see Fig. 83).

143

polished grooved axes, and bolas are artifacts shared with other Desert regions. Chisels, bells, semilunar knives, tweezers, rings, and bracelets are typical objects fashioned of copper. The dry climate minimizes deterioration of wood, bone, fiber, hide, calabash, basketry, feathers, and textiles, thus allowing an unusually complete representation of the perishable material culture. Although the population of the Puna appears to have maintained itself in part by the exchange of products with neighboring areas, relatively little acculturation resulted from these contacts. The persistence of many traits characteristic in the Valliserrana region during the initial pottery-making period is another expression of cultural retardation under the impact of severe environmental conditions.

By A.D. 1500, the Inca had expanded the borders of their Empire to embrace most of northwestern Argentina and northern Chile (Fig. 44). Highways were extended; fortresses, warehouses, and way-stations were built, and up to 90 percent of the pottery in such places is of Inca types. The inhabitants of the Desert Area were thus in some measure prepared for Spanish domination, which followed not long after.

THE PLAINS

Extensive grass-covered plains stretch eastward from the base of the cordillera, north of approximately 30 degrees in North America and south of the same latitude in South America. Although characterized by relatively slight relief, the land rises gradually toward the west. Concomitantly, average annual rainfall decreases from about 760 mm. to 380 mm. As a consequence of these differences in precipitation and elevation, the tall grass dominating the eastern plains gives way to short grass toward the west. The tall-grass zone is broken by rivers and streams with forested banks, which provide shelter from the winds that race across the plains; in the more arid short-grass prairie, springs are a typical source of water. The grassland was the habitat of large herds—bison, antelope, and deer in North America and guanaco and rhea in South America—while the wooded ravines supported a variety of small mammals and birds. In both areas, human adaptation was transformed by the introduction of the horse from Europe in the late 16th century.

The greatest difference between the northern and southern Plains is

climatic. In North America, their location in the center of the continent, remote from the ameliorating influence of the oceans, results in
extreme seasonal variation between hot summers, when the temperature
may rise to 47° C., and cold winters, when it drops well below freezing.
Although winters are warmer toward the south, no place is free of frost.
The climate of the Argentine pampa, by contrast, is moderated by the
adjacent Atlantic Ocean. The temperature for the warmest month averages around 24° C., and although winter brings frost, the average temperature remains above freezing. This milder climate might be expected
to have made the southern plains more attractive for aboriginal settlement, but present archeological information does not bear this out. A
possible explanation lies in the differential accessibility of the two areas
to centers of higher cultural development, and their consequent unequal
opportunity to acquire potentially useful innovations.

The North American Great Plains (Fig. 18, Area 5A). Little is
known of the interval between the disappearance of Paleo-Indian culture and the introduction of pottery making on the North American
Plains. It is probable that the pattern of life during this time continued
to be essentially nomadic, and small groups of hunters and gatherers
almost constantly on the move would leave little for the archeologist to
find. In especially favorable locations, which were repeatedly occupied
as winter camps, preceramic remains attest to man's continuing
presence.

The record becomes clearer with the introduction of pottery from
the Eastern Woodlands about 500 B.C. From this time onward, the inhabitants of the tall-grass plains continued to be influenced by developments taking place in the Mississippi Valley. The Hopewellian expansion is reflected between about A.D. 200 and 400 in the introduction
of maize and bean cultivation, platform pipes, copper and obsidian, pottery with rocker-stamped decoration, and innovations in burial pattern,
including the building of small earth mounds over tombs. Houses were
of perishable construction, leaving little archeological trace, but storage
pits are a common feature. Hunting and fishing still contributed importantly to the diet, as did the gathering of wild fruits, roots, seeds, and
berries.

A more pronounced cultural change took place about A.D. 1000,
probably deriving its impetus from the expanding Mississippian culture.

Large earth-lodge villages spread over the bluffs and river terraces, reflecting a more sedentary community pattern supported by the cultivation of maize, beans, and squash on the adjacent flood plain. Early earth lodges were square to rectangular in floor plan, usually 5 to 9 meters long. The sod was removed to lower the floor slightly, and four posts were erected to support the roof, which was constructed of successive layers of twigs, brush, grass, and earth. A narrow passage at one end served as the entrance and a small hole in the center of the roof allowed the exit of smoke from the fire pit below. Over the centuries, villages grew from three or four haphazardly arranged houses to between 6 and 20 dwellings; population is estimated at between 50 and 300 inhabitants. In later times, there was sometimes a surrounding defensive ditch and palisade. Bell-shaped pits, with a small opening and an expanded bottom, were used to store grain and other preservable food. The dead were buried in cemeteries or large ossuary pits adjacent to the village.

Hunting still contributed importantly to subsistence, and it is probable that at appropriate times of the year a large portion of the community set forth on expeditions to bring back a supply of bison meat to last over the winter. Bone awls and needles, stone scrapers and knives were used to dress skins and convert them into clothing, containers, and a variety of other items of daily use. Stone arrowheads, bone fishhooks, and bison scapula hoes indicate the multiple nature of subsistence activities, while shell pendants, polished stone beads and pipes, and bone gaming pieces reflect the lighter side of life. Pottery vessels with a rounded body, constricted mouth, thickened rim, and plain or cord-marked surface are characteristic. The elaborate Mississippian ceremonialism is little evident on the Plains and marked regional variation is characteristic throughout the prehistoric period.

After A.D. 1500, villages along the major watercourses increased in size to 50 or more houses, while those along lesser streams disappeared. Earth lodges became circular and larger in average diameter, some exceeding 16 meters (Figs. 91 and 92). Such evidence of increased population concentration implies intensification of agriculture, an inference also supported by proliferation in the number of storage pits per village. This period of florescence was cut short in the early 19th century, when the introduction of European diseases and the raids of equestrian hunters from the west and north devastated the village farming communities.

While the occupants of the tall grass plains were advancing toward an increasingly sedentary life, those in the western part of the area remained hunters and gatherers. Archeological evidence consists of rock shelters, cairns, stone alignments, quarries, workshops, pictographs, and campsites, identified by traces of hearths and a few scattered stone artifacts. Rings of stones are frequently encountered, some of which mark the location of tipis (conical pole and skin tents), having been used to weight down the lower border. Before the introduction of the horse, hunting ranges were limited and camps had to be moved frequently for continued accessibility to game. Dependence on hunting is reflected in the artifact inventory, which consists principally of chipped stone projectile points, knives, scrapers, and choppers, but wild plants were certainly not neglected. A few pottery vessels and soapstone bowls were also made and used.

By the time that European settlement began, acquisition of the horse had transformed the small and relatively primitive hunting bands into large tribes whose prowess in horse thievery and warfare made them the scourge of the colonists and whose spectacular feather headdresses and colorful ceremonialism dominate the popular stereotype of the American Indian. Post-European Plains culture was so marvelously adapted to the horse that it is frequently assumed to be a wholly recent development. When members of the Coronado expedition discovered the Plains in 1541, however, they encountered "people who lived like Arabs . . . in tents made of the tanned skins of the cows [bison]," who "conversed by means of signs . . . so well that there was no need of an interpreter," and who moved camp "with a lot of dogs which dragged their possessions" (Winship, 1896, pp. 504–5). The pole and buffalo-hide tipi, travois, and sign language, which are among the diagnostic elements of the historic period, were by this testimony part of the pre-horse complex. It seems probable, therefore, that rather than being a totally or even largely post-European development, equestrian hunting culture was made possible by the addition of the horse to a configuration of traits evolved during millennia of adaptation to the Plains environment. The fuel was ready; the horse was the tinder that set off the blaze.

147

Fig. 91. Earth lodge of the Omaha tribe.

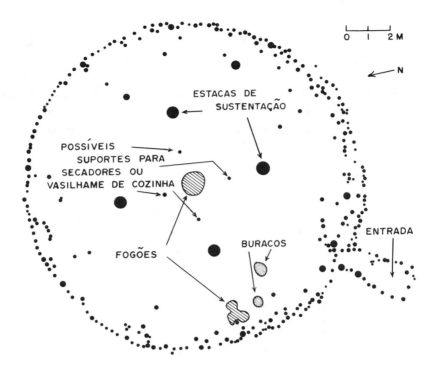

Fig. 92. Archeological remains of a post-contact earth lodge in South Dakota. The dots correspond to posts of different diameters. Small ones placed close together form the circular wall and projecting entry passage. Larger ones supported the roof. Two hearths were encountered during clearing of the floor, as well as two small pits. Four small postholes forming a square around the central hearth suggest the use of a frame similar to that constructed by the Eskimo (Fig. 100), both for suspension of cooking vessels over the fire and for drying clothing and other articles.

149

The Argentine and Uruguayan Pampa (Fig. 18, Area 5B). Whereas some 10,000 archeological sites have been reported from the North American Plains, reconstruction of the sequence of cultural development on the South American grasslands must be based on a sample less than a tenth of this size. The small amount of available data suggests the emergence of a dichotomy similar to that in North America between more sedentary pottery-making groups along the Paraná River and the coast (Fig. 87) and wandering hunters of the pampa. Shell middens are common along the shore and although some are of considerable antiquity, others were still occupied by hunting, fishing, and gathering peoples at the time of European contact. Camp and workshop sites on the pampa have produced projectile points and bola stones used in hunting; stone scrapers and knives and bone awls and punches for working hides; hammerstones, mortars, and pestles for the preparation of flour from dried fish; and worked shell and polished stone beads and pendants worn as ornaments. Simple rounded bowls and jars of pottery were manufactured in the later period and sometimes decorated by incision, drag-and-jab, zoned punctation or painting. No trace of dwellings has survived, but ethnographic sources indicate that a temporary lean-to of poles covered with mats, brush or animal skins was the typical shelter. Both primary and secondary burials are reported, without accompanying offerings.

With the exception of pottery, most of the archeological remains imply a way of life little different from that of earlier millennia and ethnographic data do not significantly alter this interpretation. The kinds of traits that predated the introduction of the horse in North America and facilitated the emergence of a more elaborate configuration there did not exist on the pampa. As a consequence, although acquisition of the horse made hunting easier and probably accelerated the pace of warfare, it did not catalyze a cultural florescence equal to that on the North American Plains.

Several groups near the Paraná River were practicing agriculture when first seen by Europeans. Although this way of life is certainly aboriginal, it may not be of great antiquity. Maize cultivation, corrugated and painted pottery, and palisaded villages, which are among the characteristic traits, did not make their appearance on the south coast of Brazil until after about A.D. 500. Their introduction to the lower

Paraná River is traceable to the expulsion of the Jesuit missions from Brazil in the 17th century.

Failure to reach a level of development comparable to that achieved in North America may be less a consequence of environment than of geography. The North American Plains are penetrated by numerous tributaries of the Mississippi River, which provided routes for the introduction of elements from the more highly developed Forest cultures. By contrast, the Paraná River system drains a region of marginal cultural significance, far removed from the climax area along the Amazon floodplain. More complex cultures existed in the Desert Area to the west, but little influence can be detected from this direction. In North America, where a similar juxtaposition of Desert and Plains environments occurs, there is also little evidence of effective communication, implying a kind of cultural incompatibility resulting from adaptation to totally different types of natural resources.

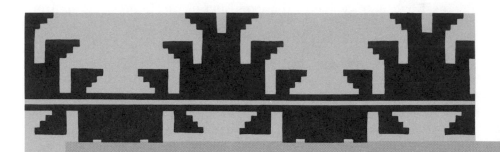

CHAPTER 5

ENVIRONMENTAL LIMITATION ON CULTURAL

COMPLEXITY: THE PACIFIC COASTS,

THE MARGINALS, AND THE ARCTIC

Where agriculture is impossible or unproductive because of deficiencies in the environment, cultural development cannot proceed beyond a relatively rudimentary level except under exceptional circumstances; even then, the possibilities are limited. In the New World, three primary types of areas fall within this category: the Pacific Coasts, which were too dry or too wet for primitive agriculture, but which provided a reliable supply of wild foods; the Marginal Areas, where wild subsistence resources were fewer and more scattered; and the Arctic, the most hostile habitat to which mankind has ever made a successful adaptation. The environmental limitations on the food supply held both population concentration and sedentariness to minimal levels in such regions, creating a social context that prevented adoption of advanced traits even if they became known. Although the cultural configurations in each area have distinctive characteristics that stem from adaptation to their specific environments, a general similarity links them not only with one another but with the hunters and gatherers who settled the hemisphere and were its only inhabitants throughout most of the prehistoric period.

THE PACIFIC COASTS

Along the Pacific coasts of the United States, Canada, and Chile, narrow strips of land are squeezed between the mountains and the sea. This geographic and topographic resemblance is enhanced by similarities in climate and vegetation. Between about 40 and 60 degrees north latitude and between about 43 and 48 degrees south latitude, the coast is a maze of islands, tortuous channels, and deep fiords. Precipitation is heavy, damp cloudy days are typical, and dense rain forest blankets the land. In addition to fish and shellfish, sea mammals such as the seal and whale are potential sources of food. Proceeding toward the equator, rainfall diminishes almost to zero, and rain forest gives way to deciduous and ultimately xerophytic vegetation. In southern California and northern Chile, rainfall is negligible or absent in certain areas. This arid portion of the coast is occupied by a low mountain range, which defines the western edge of a long valley bounded on the east by the cordillera rising to above 5000 meters. Rivers are dry except during flash floods, making irrigation difficult and minimizing the possibility of

153

agriculture without elaborate water transportation techniques.

Overriding these fundamental geographic resemblances are differences in wild food resources that played a crucial role in aboriginal cultural development. On the Northwest Coast of North America, lying principally within the boundaries of Canada, innumerable streams and two major rivers cascade from the mountains to the sea. These served as spawning ground for salmon, which constituted a subsistence resource of fantastic abundance. The adjacent seas contain halibut, cod, herring, and smelt in such numbers that they remain favored commercial fishing grounds to the present day. Seal, otter, porpoise, and whale also inhabit the waters, while deer, elk, mountain goat, and smaller mammals roam the land, providing a varied potential source of meat. Berries, nuts, and other wild plants were also bountiful in season. Farther to the south, increasing aridity brought changing vegetation, including the appearance of oaks whose prolific acorn harvest became the subsistence staple. Wild food gathering conditions were often so productive that population density could attain levels reached elsewhere only after the introduction of agriculture. The California coast, which represents only about one percent of the land north of Mexico, is estimated to have supported some ten percent of the North American population at the time of the Conquest. Villages of up to 1400 people compare favorably in size with those of agriculturalists in the adjacent Desert Area.

By contrast, wild food gathering conditions on the Chilean coast were much less auspicious. Although some of the same sea and land mammals occurred, the most productive North American resources were not duplicated. In the absence of a moderating influence equivalent to the Japan Current, which maintains temperatures in western Canada above freezing, frosts and snows accompany winter cold in Tierra del Fuego. The southern Chilean coast was also more isolated from major diffusion paths, with the result that few new techniques, customs or ideas became available to the inhabitants. The environmental limitations on increased population concentration are sufficiently severe, however, to make it doubtful that greater accessibility would have permitted a significantly higher level of cultural development.

The North Pacific Coast (Fig. 18, Area 6A). Between 2000 and 1000 B.C., increasing specialization toward exploitation of the most productive kinds of local food resources begins to be evident on the Pacific

Coast of North America. In the southern portion of the area, villages are larger than in earlier times and possibly more sedentary. The appearance of stone mortars with basketry tops, a utensil for processing acorns, indicates concentration on this plant food. The continued importance of hunting, fishing, and shellfish gathering is implied by a variety of chipped stone implements, in addition to barbed harpoon points. Stone was less utilized than in earlier times, its place taken by bone, which was employed for the manufacture of whistles and tubes as well as awls.

After the beginning of the Christian era, stronger contrasts emerged between the shore dwellers, who depended heavily on marine resources, and the inhabitants of the central valley, who concentrated on plant foods. Along the seacoast, specialized tools, such as circular shell fishhooks, burins, steatite bowls, large mortars and pestles, obsidian projectile points with serrated edges, and a wide variety of ornaments of stone, bone, and shell, become characteristic. Incised bird-bone tubes, tubular steatite pipes, and polished stone sculpture (Fig. 93) also occur. Dome-shaped, circular houses, 4 to 7 meters in diameter, were constructed of poles covered with grass. Each village also had an earth-covered, semisubterranean sweat house. Traces of influences from the Desert Area to the southeast can be detected, particularly in the introduction of pottery, but differences in environmental resources and the closeness of adaptation to wild food subsistence apparently made most items of Southwestern Desert culture irrelevant or incompatible.

In the interior valley, technology remained less complex. Seed grinding tools, chipped stone knives, scrapers, and projectile points changed form through time, but fulfilled similar functions. Basketry, cordage, and other perishable artifacts have been preserved in dry caves, attesting to the importance of these kinds of objects and to the skill that was attained in their manufacture. By the time of European contact, basketry had been developed to a high degree of artistry and versatility and in the absence of cotton was used even for the manufacture of certain articles of dress.

While the arid portion of the Pacific Coast supported a dense population in late aboriginal times, it was the wetter northern sector where the cultural climax occurred. Here, a remarkably prolific supply of wild food provided the prerequisite subsistence stability and Asiatic influ-

Fig. 93. Killer whale carved from steatite and inlaid with shell disks, from the late period on the southern California coast. Length is about 10 cm.

Fig. 94. Haida thunderbird design, showing the bifurcation of animals to permit inclusion of all features in a single view that was characteristic of Northwest Coast art.

156

ences may have furnished the catalyst for development of the striking Northwest Coast cultural configuration, particularly renowned for its distinctive and colorful art style (Fig. 94). As early as 1000 B.C., the specialized exploitation of sea mammals can be inferred from the presence of projectile points of shell, bone, antler, and ground slate, some with smooth edges, others barbed along one side. In the wet climate, few other artifacts are preserved except small nephrite adzes and chisels, which indicate the beginnings of woodworking, and ornaments like polished stone labrets and ear spools. By 200 B.C., large adzes and stone mauls become increasingly common. Such tools were employed to hew planks for house construction and in the manufacture of dugout canoes, implying the development of these basic ingredients of later Northwest Coast culture by this time. Larger population concentrations and an increased variety of luxury goods, such as ornaments of native copper, quantities of beads, and examples of stone sculpture, reflect the accentuation of differences in status and wealth. Small earth and stone burial mounds about one meter high, constructed over a single partly cremated burial, may date from this time, but the rarity of grave goods makes their temporal identification uncertain.

Archeological sites dated between A.D. 1200–1600 provide indirect evidence of some perishable elements of historic Northwest Coast culture. Heavy antler and bone wedges and stone mauls used in wood working are common. Zoomorphic clubs, tubular steatite pipes, and stone bowls exhibit what must be a pale reflection of artistic and technical skills expressed in perishable materials. If the culture had not survived to be described by European travelers and later by ethnographers, the material remains would be insufficient to permit reconstruction of the social stratification, complicated rules of economic competition, mythology, art style, and ceremonialism that have intrigued all who have become aware of their existence. Although contrasts of such an extreme nature between the content of a living culture and the surviving archeological remains may not be typical, this example underscores the limitations of the archeological record and emphasizes the fact that even where preservation is relatively good, much more once existed than has been left behind.

The South Pacific Coast (Fig. 18, Area 6B). One of the difficulties in correlating the archeological sequences of the Chilean coast with those of neighboring areas is the scarcity of absolute dates. Nonceramic sites abound in the arid northern region, some of which are of considerable antiquity but others of which probably reflect the survival of groups with simple technology until recent times. As in North America, increasing specialization on seafood resources is evident in the appearance of shell fishhooks and bone harpoon heads, while small stemmed stone points were used on darts and other projectiles. Stone bowls are characteristic, as are scrapers and other percussion-flaked stone tools. With the passage of time, thorn fishhooks replaced those of shell, harpoon heads assumed different forms, triangular projectile points became popular, and new kinds of stone artifacts, including bola stones and cigar-shaped sinkers, imply changes in hunting and fishing methods.

Around the beginning of the Christian era, agriculture, pottery making, weaving, coiled basketry, metallurgy, and other Central Andean traits were introduced to the north coast. In the Atacama region (Fig. 87), settled life appears suddenly in well developed form, indicating intrusion from elsewhere, and the presence of Cienaga pottery implies that the source is the Valliserrana region of the adjacent Desert Area. Conditions favorable to agriculture were restricted to scattered oases, where maize, gourds, potatoes, and beans were raised in limited quantities. Small villages composed of rectangular stone-walled houses enclosed by a defensive wall occupied rocky outcrops near land suitable for farming. Subterranean storage bins and granaries in the house corners, as well as large mortars and metates, attest to dependence on maize. Plain or polished red ceramics are associated with polished stone axes, copper bracelets, gold plaques, bone spatulas, tubular pipes, and wooden tablets. Several types of graves occur, including stone-lined pits and pit-and-chamber forms. In the Arica region, various kinds of objects were manufactured in miniature for burial purposes, such as pottery vessels, bows and arrows, rafts and paddles, reed mats, and loom sticks. Gourd containers, composite combs, spindles, adzes, and coca bags are other items frequently placed with the dead.

Around A.D. 700, strong Tiahuanaco influence is manifested in religious art motifs (trophy heads, condors, felines, human figures holding scepters) and in luxury goods, such as mosaic incrustations, engraved bone tubes, embossed gold keros (flaring goblets), and cast metal objects. The post-Tiahuanaco period, after about A.D. 1000, is characterized initially by regionalization and adaptation to local environmental situations. Immediately prior to the Inca conquest, fortified villages became common, implying that the process of political development evident in the adjacent Desert region was under way here as well.

The Transversal Valleys of central Chile were more isolated geographically from the Andean highlands and followed a more independent pattern of development. Their initial pottery, however, exhibits a number of Andean features absent in the east, including stirrup spouts, bridge handles, and post-fired painting, suggesting a contact by sea with the Peruvian coast. Subsequent innovations reflect influence from the Valliserrana, among them polychrome painting. Isolation seems to have increased after about A.D. 700 to judge from the absence of Tiahuanaco elements or introductions from the flourishing Tafí and Aguada cultures on the opposite side of the cordillera.

In the more humid zone to the south, cultural retardation is even more apparent. The prodigious fish supply of the North American sea and rivers was missing, so that food getting was much more time consuming and laborious. As a result, settlements remained small and houses were of primitive and impermanent construction (Fig. 95). Stone and shell adzes were used to cut planks for boats, which were so unseaworthy that constant bailing was required to keep them afloat. The satisfaction of daily needs left little time for other activities and only special and temporary circumstances permitted gatherings larger than extended family groups. In contrast to the situation on the Northwest Coast of North America, the extreme simplicity of archeological remains in Tierra del Fuego accurately reflects the cultural simplicity of the area, whose primitive inhabitants were vividly described by Charles Darwin in 1832:

These were the most abject and miserable creatures I anywhere beheld. . . . Their country is a broken mass of wild rocks, lofty hills, and useless forests: and these are viewed through mists and endless storms. The habitable land is reduced to the stones on the beach; in search of food they are compelled unceasingly to wander from spot to spot. . . . At night, five or six human beings, naked and scarcely protected from the wind and rain of this tempestuous climate, sleep on the wet ground coiled up like animals. Whenever it is low water, winter or summer, night or day, they must rise to pick shellfish from the rocks; and the women either dive to collect sea-eggs,

159

Fig. 95. *Alacaluf camp on the southern Chilean coast. The huts are oval and average about 4.0 by 2.3 meters and 1.8 meters high. The pole framework is covered with sea lion skins, bark, and ferns. An oval hearth occupies the center of the floor.*

or sit patiently in their canoes, and with a baited hair-line without any hook, jerk out little fish. If a seal is killed, or the floating carcass of a putrid whale discovered, it is a feast; and such miserable food is assisted by a few tasteless berries and fungi. . . .

Foreshadowing modern cultural ecological thinking by more than a century, Darwin saw the Fuegian way of life as adaptive, given the limitations of the environment:

Whilst beholding these savages, one asks, whence they come? What could have tempted, or what change compelled a tribe of men to leave the fine regions of the north, to travel down the Cordillera or backbone of America, to invent and build canoes, . . . and then to enter on one of the most inhospitable countries within the limits of the globe? Although such reflections must at first seize on the mind, yet we may feel sure that they are partly erroneous. There is no reason to believe that the Fuegians decrease in number; therefore we must suppose that they enjoy a sufficient share of happiness, of whatever kind it may be, to render life worth having. Nature by making habit omnipotent, and its effects hereditary, has fitted the Fuegian to the climate and the productions of his miserable country (1871, pp. 213, 215–216).

THE MARGINALS

Certain interior portions of the New World are unsuitable for intensive agriculture for one or more of a variety of reasons, such as too much or too little moisture, too short a growing season, infertile soil, or too low an average temperature. In some of these areas, human habitation was dependent on intensive exploitation of wild food resources; in others, incipient agriculture could provide supplemental rations. Subsistence limitations kept population density very low, and ways of life developed during the Transitional Period were preserved until European contact.

In North America, continental width increases toward the pole with the result that a large land mass stretches into the latitudes where shortness of the growing season makes agriculture impossible (Fig. 18, Area 7A). Hunting, fishing, and gathering resources are good but not concentrated, so that small groups could support themselves only by remaining relatively mobile and exploiting a variety of seasonal foods. A similar situation existed in the plateau and basin area of the north-western United States, a region of hot summers and cold winters, of extreme altitude variation and limited rainfall, which has been described as one of the most difficult environments in the world for human use.

Because continental width diminishes in South America as latitude increases, areas with marginal agricultural potential are smaller and more scattered. The largest is the upland region of eastern Brazil, where erratic fluctuation in annual rainfall makes farming undependable (Fig. 18, Area 7B). In the swampy lowland of the Gran Chaco, portions of which lie in Paraguay, Bolivia, and Brazil, hunting, fishing, and gathering also remained the primary subsistence pattern until post-European times.

The Marginal Areas have attracted little attention from archeologists for an obvious reason: The cultures occupying them were poorly equipped with tools and utensils of a nonperishable nature, and those that did exist were relatively undistinctive. Moreover, the wandering way of life prevented the concentration of remains, so that sites are difficult to find and generally produce a minimum of evidence (Fig. 96). The best known archeological sequence is from the North American basin-plateau, where a generalized "desert" type of culture persisted from late Paleo-Indian to modern times. Changes can be observed in the size and form of projectile points and in the appearance and disappearance of specific kinds of shell ornaments, bone tools, or pottery, but these are minor alterations in a cultural configuration of great stability.

Since the Marginal way of life existed until recently in parts of North and South America, the archeological reconstruction can be tested against ethnographic descriptions. Steward's (1938) pioneering investigation of cultural ecology among the Paiute and Shoshone in northwestern Nevada not only provides details on the subsistence round, but also shows how the nature of the resources determined the general cultural configuration.

In this mountain and valley habitat, wild food resources were extremely varied, but localized and often available during only a few days or weeks. Productivity fluctuated not only regionally but also from one year to the next. A family normally exploited an area about 30 kilo-

162

Fig. 96. *Paiute camp in southern Utah, photographed a century ago during the Powell expedition. The pole and brush construction is typical of the temporary shelters utilized by wandering hunting and gathering groups the world over.*

meters in radius, and utilized between 30 and 80 species of plants in the form of seeds, roots, berries, or greens. Trips of more than 100 kilometers were often made, however, for hunting or because local harvests failed. Each biological family was a self-supporting unit: the women gathered plant products while the men hunted. Both caught rodents and insects (especially crickets and grasshoppers). A generalized seasonal round was followed, beginning with harvesting of green shoots in early spring, continuing with seed gathering in early summer, roots and berries in late summer, and pine nuts in early fall. Stored pine nuts were the principal winter fare, supplemented by game. Fish were obtained from some rivers and water fowl from the lakes. Antelope, rabbit, deer, and mountain sheep were hunted communally, and involved cooperation between up to two dozen families for a week or more. When pine nuts were plentiful or a surplus of food was provided by a rabbit or antelope drive, several families were able temporarily to remain together and to hold festivals, which included dancing, gambling, and socializing with friends and relatives rarely seen except on such occasions. When this hunting and gathering subsistence pattern is generalized and plotted on a map (Fig. 97), it is reminiscent of the way of life reconstructed from archeological evidence left by inhabitants of the Tehuacán Valley in central Mexico during the Transitional Period, between 6800 and 5000 B.C. (Fig. 10).

Students of American Indian culture have long noted that the most primitive peoples of North and South America possess a considerable number of cultural elements that are absent or sporadic in the intervening region. Nordenskiold (1931), who devoted the greatest attention to this phenomenon, compiled a list of 64 such traits, which has been expanded by other investigators (e.g., Cooper, 1941; Métraux, 1939). Although some are of a technological nature, such as bark containers and fish glue, the overwhelming majority are in the realms of mythology, music, religion, ritual, and recreation. Some legends, including a series dealing with the exploits of a trickster, are amazingly uniform. The best explanation for the existence of these traits in such widely separated regions is that they formed part of the basic culture spread over both continents during the Paleo-Indian Period and have survived only among those groups whose general way of life is a perpetuation from that remote time.

164

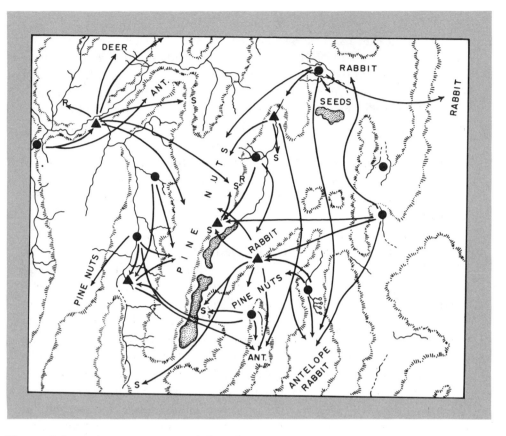

Fig. 97. Schematic representation of the subsistence and settlement pattern developed by Paiute and Shoshone hunting and gathering groups in the mountains of northwestern Nevada. Circles and triangles indicate winter camps, which were located in sheltered places where a good fuel supply was available. During the height of winter, the people lived on game and stored pine nuts. Arrows symbolize movements during the spring, summer, and fall to regions where roots (R), seeds (S), and other seasonal plant foods could be obtained, and to valleys where deer and rabbit were hunted. Hunting was generally a communal activity, which permitted members of different families to camp together for several days or weeks. The triangles designate villages where festivals were held.

The only type of environment without a South American counterpart is the Arctic (Fig. 18, Area 8), the last refuge of the vast ice sheets that once covered much of North America. In this forbidding region, which extends northward from the tree line (about 60 degrees north latitude), seasons are marked by changes not only in temperature but in illumination. Between sunset in late November and sunrise in early February, the icy landscape is shrouded in night. In midsummer, by contrast, one day blends into the following one, the temperature rises above freezing, and widespread melting transforms the firm tundra into an impassable bog. Although it appears hostile to an outsider, the Arctic sustains a varied and relatively abundant fauna, including seal, walrus, whales, polar bears, caribou, elk, small game, birds, and fish.

This unique and demanding environment, extending some 4800 km. from the Bering Strait to Greenland, is occupied by the Eskimo, who differ racially, culturally, and linguistically from the other inhabitants of the New World. Their cultural roots appear to lie in the Arctic Small-Tool Tradition, which appeared in the Bering Strait region after 5000 B.C. The name derives from the small size of characteristic stone tools, which were produced from blades by fine pressure flaking. The technique of manufacture and the presence of specific implements like burins, microblades, and side blades, are characteristics that ally this culture with the Eurasian Mesolithic and identify it as a late variant of the Mesolithic way of life. The absence of evidence for permanent shelters in sites of this period in the Bering Sea region suggests that sea mammal hunting was a summer activity, and that winters were passed in more sheltered places in the interior where caribou could be killed.

The inception of fully maritime Eskimo culture, characterized by primary year-round dependence on sea mammals, is implied by the appearance of the Old Bering Sea and related complexes about 1000 B.C. Rectangular stone-floored houses about 6 meters square were constructed with driftwood near the beach. Heat conservation was enhanced by an entrance passage up to 5 meters long. Since the permafrost allows no decay, innumerable by-products of daily life are preserved in the habitation refuse. In addition to chipped chert and rubbed slate points and knives, slate ulus or semilunar knives, stone drills, scrapers, and adzes, archeologists have encountered quantities of carved bone and ivory objects intermixed with food remains consisting principally of sea mammal, bird, and fish bones. Barbed harpoon points, snow picks, wedges, awls, needles and needle cases, buttons, pendants, combs, ice creepers, spoons, and buckets of ivory and bone were often decorated with distinctive curvilinear patterns formed by two or three closely spaced and precisely drawn parallel lines (Fig. 98). Pottery with linear-stamped and check-stamped surfaces appears about 500 B.C. on the northern shores of the Bering Sea; although allied by technique of surface treatment with the widespread Woodland stamped ceramic tradition, this Eskimo pottery is too recent to have served as a stepping stone in the diffusion from Asia to eastern North America. In the Arctic, pottery never competed successfully with containers of stone and skin, and became thicker and cruder with the passage of time.

The site of Ipiutak near Point Hope, Alaska, represents maritime Eskimo culture at about the beginning of the Christian era. More than 600 houses were arranged in a series of rows over a kilometer long. They were 3 to 6 meters square, with rounded corners, and had walls and roofs constructed of logs covered with sod. Earth benches along the sides served for sleeping. Inland from the village was a large cemetery covering some 4 kilometers, containing two kinds of interment. Some individuals were placed in log coffins with few grave goods; others occupied shallow depressions probably once covered with logs, and were accompanied by numerous elaborately carved ivory objects. These include not only practical items such as snow goggles, harpoon sockets, and knife handles, but ritual elements like parts of masks, linked chains, and sculptures of real and mythical animals, all manufactured with great skill and artistry. The application of artificial ivory eyes, nose plug, and mouth cover to the corpse to prevent escape of the soul, as well as the presence of linked chains and swivels, indicate that religious practices still observed in Siberia were already developed by this time.

During the first eleven centuries of the present era, the Bering Strait maritime variety of Eskimo culture spread up the Arctic coast as far as Point Barrow. As the distinctive art style decayed, a number of useful items were added to the already crowded inventory of tools and weapons. Notable among the latter were slat armor and the composite sinew-

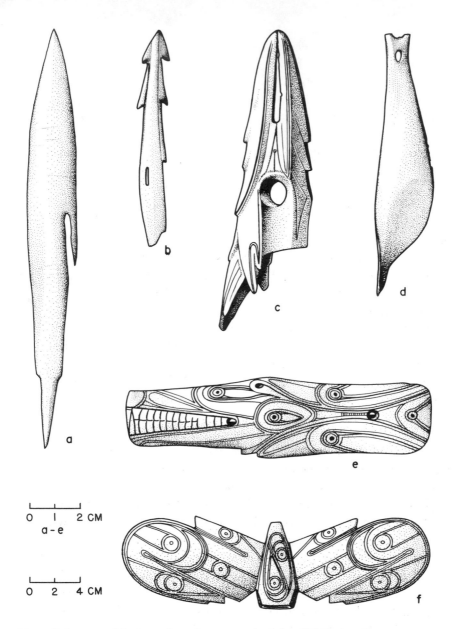

Fig. 98. Ivory and bone tools and ornaments of the Old Bering Sea culture. a, arrowhead; b, bird dart point; c, harpoon head; d, fishline sinker; e, ornament; f, winged object.

Fig. 99. An Eskimo masked figure dressed for a ceremony. He holds a seal spear in one hand and a scraper in the other. An inflated sealskin buoy is carried on his back. The sealskin mask is decorated to simulate tattooing. This drawing is based on a sketch made by Franz Boas during field work in the Davis Strait region in 1883–4.

backed bow with its accompanying wrenches and wrist guard, introduced from Siberia about A.D. 800. Other significant Siberian imports
were two types of large sleds, which supplemented existing smaller
sleds and toboggans and probably mark the introduction of dog trac-
tion. A crucial element of maritime Eskimo culture was light-weight
tailored clothing, sewn from caribou, bird or polar bear skin, which was
designed to provide both the insulation necessary at low temperatures
and ventilation for escape of moisture from the skin and inner garments.
Neglect of the latter feature allows the accumulation of ice, and ignor-
ance of its importance caused the death of many early European explorers of the Polar region.

While the inhabitants of the Bering Strait were becoming increasingly specialized to the hunting of walrus and other sea mammals,
eastern Canada, Newfoundland, and Greenland were occupied by peo-

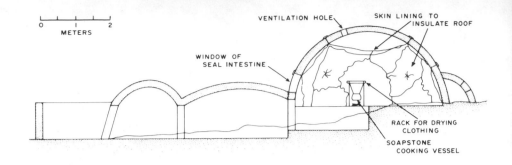

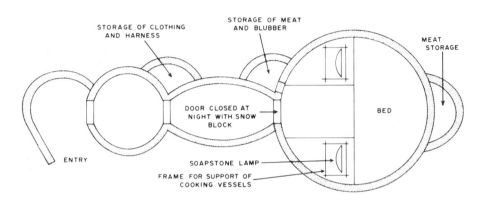

Fig. 100. *Diagram made by Franz Boas of a two-family igloo in use in 1883–4. The main dwelling is entered through a passage composed of circular and ovoid sections connected by doorways 75–90 cm. high. The long entrance, along with the change in floor level, aids in keeping cold air out. Construction is done by two men, one who cuts blocks 90 to 120 cm. long, 60 cm. wide, and 15 to 20 cm. thick, and the other who places them in the wall. The initial row is a complete circle; when finished, the upper edge is cut on a slope so that the blocks in succeeding rows assume a slanting position that provides support on the bottom and one side. Inward inclination increases with height and the final roof blocks are inserted from inside. An igloo 2 meters in diameter and 1.5 meters high can be constructed in two hours. In larger structures, like that depicted, the vault is lined with skins held in place by a cord through the snow wall, secured on the exterior by a toggle.*

The shelf at the rear is the bed. Tentpoles, oars, and other pieces of wood are laid on the snow and covered with a thick layer of brush. Heavy deerskins are spread over this, and another deerskin serves as a blanket. Clothing is removed and placed at the edge of the shelf as a pillow. The "lamps," which burn seal oil, must be tended frequently to prevent excessive smoking. They generate sufficient heat to keep the **interior temperature between 8° and 18° C.**

ple of the Dorset complex. The material culture inventory combines tiny arrowheads, microblades, miniature needles, and harpoon heads derived from the Arctic Small-Tool Tradition with new elements, such as multi-barbed bone fish spears, snow knives, ulu-like bone knives, and bone sledge runners. Circular or rectangular houses with stone and turf walls occur at some sites; at others, perishable structures of poles covered with skins may have been used. Although seal was the principal staple, birds, salmon, small game, and caribou were exploited at different seasons. In contrast to the Eskimos and most Indians, the Dorset people did not have dogs.

The striking homogeneity of modern Eskimo culture derives from the pan-Arctic spread about A.D. 1200 of the Thule culture, which seems to have developed in the central Canadian Arctic. Millennia of coping with a hostile environment and the circumpolar interchange of ideas brought into being many inventions of remarkable efficiency. The Eskimo lamp, which provides a maximum of heat from a minimum of fuel, is one example. Another is two-layered clothing, which improved insulation without adding bulk. The ingenious use of nonedible parts of animals is manifest in many articles of daily use, from kayaks to bladder floats (Fig. 99). In fact, if all objects made from skins, bone, and ivory were eliminated, little would be left of Eskimo material culture. The dog sled remains the most reliable means of transportation over snow and frozen water. The igloo provides life-saving emergency shelter on trackless wastes of ice (Fig. 100). In short, although modern Eskimo culture incorporates many Old World elements of considerable antiquity, it is a unique and recent product of cultural evolution, not a survival of an ancient way of life.

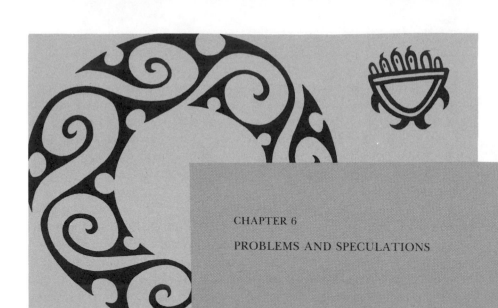

CHAPTER 6

PROBLEMS AND SPECULATIONS

A review of cultural development in prehistoric America in the context of 8 general types of environment brings out two significant facts. The first is that strikingly parallel configurations evolved in similar habitats in North and South America. Resemblances occur in subsistence pattern, house type, village composition, tools and utensils, religious symbols, art styles, ceremonial practices, and numerous other kinds of features. The second is that cultural evolution did not proceed at the same rate in different kinds of environments, with the result that by the time of European contact widely discrepant levels of complexity had emerged from the common denominator provided by the hemisphere-wide dispersal of the Pre-Projectile Point and Paleo-Indian hunters and gatherers. At one extreme were the civilizations of the Inca, Maya, and Aztec, which excelled those of contemporary Europe in several aspects of technology, calendrical accuracy, and scale of urbanism. At the other extreme were the Marginals, whose way of life remained a reasonable facsimile of that prevalent during the Transitional Period, some 6 to 8 millennia earlier. Since the goal of science is not simply to describe but to understand, how are we to explain both the resemblances in cultural development that emerged in environmentally similar portions of the Americas and the marked differences in level of complexity extant at the time of European contact?

We can begin by assuming that the explanation will not be simple. All of the principal variables—soil, topography, climate, flora, fauna, and culture—are complex phenomena resulting from millennia of interaction between physical, evolutionary, and historical factors, few of which are completely understood and many of which remain unknown. In addition, each variable is continually influencing and being influenced by all the others, vastly increasing the complexity of the process. Because so little is known, it is possible to identify only a few of the more obvious factors involved.

If the peopling of the hemisphere has been correctly reconstructed, one source of similarity is the survival of elements that formed part of the culture of the earliest immigrants. This explanation was proposed many years ago to account for numerous duplications between non-agricultural groups in North and South America in myths, games, music, religion, and certain kinds of material objects, among them sewed bark containers and three-feathered arrows. These elements were modified or replaced where agriculture and increasingly settled life opened new possibilities and made older practices obsolete. In the Marginal Areas, where hunting and gathering subsistence patterns continued little changed, they remained a functional part of the cultural complex.

Another important cause of similarity is diffusion. Unlike biological innovations, which are generally transmitted genetically, and consequently require many generations to become common in a population, cultural innovations are disseminated by learning. Theoretically, therefore, an invention or discovery can spread over an extensive area in a short time. The apparently rapid dissemination of the Paleo-Indian projectile point technology over most of the hemisphere in a few centuries is an outstanding example. Cultural exchange between Mesoamerica and the Andes during the Formative has been amply documented (Ford, 1969), and throughout the prehistoric period influences from the Nuclear Areas remained a primary stimulus for cultural advance in other parts of the Americas. Many traits were undoubtedly so greatly modified during integration into the recipient culture that their origin has been masked and they have been erroneously attributed to independent invention or convergence. The difficulty of distinguishing between these alternatives underlies many of the disagreements about the existence of connections between Olmec and Chavín, Adena-Hopewell and Mesoamerica, and Mesoamerica and southeast Asia. Other elements are sufficiently distinctive that their unitary origin is indisputable; traits such as the litter as a symbol of rank (Figs. 34, 49, 74), the preservation of human heads as trophies (Figs. 39, 50, 51, 67, 75, 81, 89), and the ritual significance of felines (Figs. 19, 20, 28, 35, 38, 45, 46, 47, 50, 51, 53, 64, 65, 66, 76, 88) impart a fundamental unity to New World culture.

Since independent invention has long been an acceptable explanation for the occurrence of similar traits in noncontiguous regions, it deserves brief comment. Its popularity derives from two assumptions: (1) that human beings are so inventive that they are likely to develop the same kinds of traits repeatedly, and (2) that many of the duplications involve such simple concepts or techniques that reinvention is highly probable, if not inevitable. There is no justification, however, for assuming that an idea that seems self-evident to us was equally obvious to someone who had never been exposed to it. On the contrary, the evi-

174

dence indicates that many "simple" inventions originated only once. For example, when the first appearance in different parts of the Americas of such commonplace pottery characteristics as red-slipped surfaces and rounded bowl shape is plotted as a function of geography, a sloping chronological pattern emerges that clearly indicates their dissemination from a single point of origin (Ford, 1969). The same kind of pattern is exhibited by many decorative techniques, more elaborate vessel forms, and other cultural elements, indicating that their widespread occurrence is the result of diffusion and not multiple reinvention.

To deny that independent invention is a probable explanation for many kinds of resemblances does not imply, of course, that it never occurs. When the efficiency of an object, such as an ax, depends upon a combination of form, size, weight, and other characteristics, independent achievement of a similar result can be expected. The availability of the same kinds of raw materials for the satisfaction of similar requirements may also cause independent duplications. Nevertheless, as more data accumulate, they make it increasingly evident that independent invention is an uncommon explanation for cultural resemblances that are not clearly tied to adaptive requirements, and that its occurrence must be demonstrated rather than taken for granted.

Diffusion never operates in a vacuum; rather, its action is facilitated, impeded, or distorted by the geographical context and cultural composition of both the donor and the recipient configurations. Let us consider first some of the most relevant geographical factors. The most obvious is proximity, since the closer two groups are to one another, the more opportunity there will be for exchange. It often happens, however, that communication is hampered by physical barriers, such as deserts or mountains, or by discontinuities in environment. The former type of obstacle delayed the transition from food gathering to food production in the Deserts for millennia in spite of their proximity to the Nuclear Areas. Differences in the ecological character of the Deserts and the Plains, or the Deserts and the Pacific Coasts, are largely responsible for divergent cultural development in these contiguous regions. The importance of environmental compatibility for the successful dissemination of many kinds of traits is even more clearly illustrated by the Forests. Although the Eastern Woodlands do not adjoin Mesoamerica, influences passed to them far more readily than they did from the Andean Area to the Amazonian lowlands, which share a long frontier.

Level of development is another significant factor in determining the amount of influence that one culture has upon another. Every culture is a highly integrated configuration and must maintain its integration to remain viable. It thus possesses mechanisms for rejection of incompatible and potentially disruptive innovations (just as an animal has defense mechanisms against infection), and generally admits only those products of diffusion that are harmonious. Among relatively simple cultures, such as the Marginals, the "filter" is very fine and little passes through. As cultural complexity increases, a wider variety of innovations can be accommodated, culminating in the fantastic diversity surrounding us today.

Other things being equal, receptivity to influence seems to be inversely related to the similarity in level of development of the cultures involved. During the early Formative Period, when agriculture made the adoption of the same general kind of settled village life possible in many parts of the Americas, technological, ceremonial, and artistic innovations compatible with this new type of community pattern were able to spread rapidly over long distances. As disparities in level of complexity became increasingly pronounced, however, the range of dissemination became correspondingly reduced. Toward the end of the prehistoric period, conquest became a more effective method than diffusion for expanding the geographical distribution of more highly developed configurations into regions where the indigenous culture remained too primitive to accept piecemeal advanced types of traits.

Failure to consider the context within which diffusion operates is a major reason for the vigor of disputes over the existence of precolumbian transpacific contacts. Attention has been concentrated on details of the traits and on their temporal and spatial distributions, and the archeological record is generally too incomplete to provide the evidence necessary for an unequivocal decision. The fact that the course of cultural development on the eastern and western margins of the Pacific was sufficiently synchronic to provide a favorable context for diffusion is rarely taken into consideration in spite of its relevance. For example, the fact that an immigrant from western Japan around 3000 B.C. would have encountered on coastal Ecuador a way of life similar to that he had known at home increases the probability that Jomon technological,

176

religious, or social elements would have been compatible with the indigenous Ecuadorian culture, although this would not necessarily have ensured their adoption. Similarly, when agriculture was securely established in the Nuclear Areas, new forms of ritual, symbols of status, specialized ceremonial structures, forms of personal adornment, and other cultural elaborations became possible. Outside influences, whether from other parts of the Americas or across the ocean, would have had a better chance for adoption at this time than at almost any other period. The evidence of a clustering of the appearance of Asiatic-like innovations at a few points in Mesoamerican and Andean prehistory seems likely to reflect such differences in receptivity.

Even more controversial than the possibility of transpacific influence is transatlantic contact. Here, the marked disparity in level of cultural development between the donor and receiver areas would have created a severe obstacle to acceptance of innovations. The donors have been postulated as Phoenicians, Greeks, Egyptians, and other groups of Mediterranean or European origin, all of whom possessed much more advanced cultures than existed anywhere along the Atlantic coasts of the Americas or on the Caribbean islands. Consequently, if a ship from such an origin reached the New World, its occupants could have had little if any permanent impact on the aboriginal inhabitants. A few glass, stone, or metal objects might have been traded, but the probability of finding any of them is slight. Only the Vikings appear to have left archeologically detectible settlements, but they made no impact on the aboriginal hunting and gathering tribes of the region. While this marked contrast in level of complexity makes it doubtful that transatlantic contacts played a significant role in American prehistory, a few puzzles such as the appearance of the Old Copper Culture during the late Archaic of the Great Lakes region and the resemblance between Woodland pottery and contemporary European ceramics suggest that some influences may have entered the hemisphere from the east.

If receptivity or resistance to innovations is determined primarily by the compatibility of the new trait with the recipient culture, then it becomes important to understand how cultural differences arise. The principal cause appears to be adaptation to the special characteristics of a particular environment. Every species including *Homo sapiens* must achieve a minimal level of food intake, shelter, and reproduction to

survive, and the conditions under which these requirements are fulfilled are set by the environment. Man entered the New World equipped
with a cultural inventory that permitted him to occupy all but the most
extreme habitats and his success in adapting to a wide range of climates and food resources is reflected in the nearly universal distribution of Paleo-Indian remains over the hemisphere.

Even during the peopling of the Americas, selective exploitation of
subsistence resources was probably beginning to occur; in the Transitional Period, adaptation to the special properties of local environments
was certainly under way. Except under the most rigorous conditions,
several alternative "strategies" were always potentially available, and
the archeological record as well as evidence from surviving unacculturated groups both indicate that variations in cultural pattern developed even where hunting and gathering remained the sole subsistence
resource. By the time of European contact, gross differences in level
of complexity were characteristic of the 8 principal environmental
regions. The Nuclear Areas had achieved civilization; the Forest,
Desert, and Intermediate Areas were occupied by village farmers, sometimes temporarily integrated into larger religious or political configurations; the Plains vacillated on the border line between nomadic and
sedentary life; the Pacific Coast, Marginal, and Arctic Areas continued
to support generalized or specialized hunting and gathering economies.
If the principal reason for these disparate expressions of cultural climax
is environmental, then it becomes necessary to ask what aspect of the
environment is the critical factor.

It has often been asserted that the acquisition of culture liberated
Homo sapiens from environmental constraints and superficial observa-
tion suggests this to be true. Man has been able to live in almost every
terrestrial habitat and to create urban centers in deserts, forests or grasslands, in equatorial or subarctic climates, at sea level or at high elevations. Furthermore, his technology now permits him to bring water to
deserts and remove it from swamps; to produce cool air in tepid regions
and artificial heat in frigid ones; to level hills, change the course of
rivers, convert forests into pastures, and exterminate numerous species
of animals. These impressive technological feats, however, do not affect the physical and biological processes that have ruled the biosphere
for at least half a billion years. Man evolved in the same way as other

178

species, and his survival depends upon his ability to maintain primary biological functions. Culture has multiplied the means by which these requirements can be satisfied, but increasingly sophisticated subsistence activities are often more rather than less vulnerable to natural hazards. Under favorable conditions agriculture provides a far more abundant, concentrated, and reliable food supply than wild plants and animals; if predators, storms, or diseases unexpectedly deplete the anticipated harvest, however, the risk of famine is greatly increased.

It has long been recognized that the domestication of plants was the crucial step in cultural evolution. Without agriculture, mankind would still be living as he was when he first entered the Americas. Furthermore, the level of development of any particular culture is closely correlated with the proportion of the diet derived from cultivated plants (Harner, 1970). It follows, therefore, that the most significant aspect of the environment for cultural evolution is its agricultural potential. From this viewpoint, 4 general types of environments can be distinguished:

Type 1, where agriculture is impossible because temperature, aridity, soil composition, altitude, topography, latitude, or some other natural factor inhibits the growth or maturation of domesticated plants. Major New World regions with these limitations are the Arctic, most of the Marginal Areas, and parts of the Pacific Coasts. Type 1 enclaves, in the form of high mountains, swamps, salt flats, and other kinds of uncultivatable terrain, also occur in areas otherwise suitable for agricultural exploitation.

Type 2, where agricultural productivity is limited to a relatively low level by climatic factors causing rapid depletion of soil fertility. Amazonia is the principal example, but parts of the Intermediate Area also belong here. Slash-and-burn or shifting cultivation, in which fields are abandoned after about 3 years production, is the typical method of farming.

Type 3, where relatively high crop yields can be obtained indefinitely from the same plot of land with fertilization, fallowing, crop rotation, and other kinds of soil restorative measures, or in more arid regions by irrigation. The Forests (except Amazonia), Deserts, Plains, and parts of the Nuclear, Intermediate, and Pacific Coast Areas fall into this category.

Type 4, where little or no specialized knowledge is required to achieve and maintain a stable level of agricultural productivity. In the Americas, this situation appears to have existed to a significant extent only in parts of the Andean Area and Mesoamerica (Meggers, 1954).

If it be granted that the differing agricultural potential of the environment is the crucial factor in explaining the origin, development, and distribution of cultures, the situation in the New World at the time of European contact makes it clear that the potentiality of a particular type of environment will not inevitably be realized. The reason is that the immediate goal of adaptation, whether biological or cultural, is to maximize the probability of survival of a population while simultaneously minimizing the likelihood of permanent damage to the environment from overexploitation. In every situation, there are usually several methods of satisfying this requirement, and which of these materialize and are perpetuated depends on a variety of factors of environmental and cultural origin. Some configurations become so well integrated with the total ecosystem that they persist indefinitely unless climatic change or cultural disturbance destroys the equilibrium. If such a crisis occurs, the outcome will depend on the cultural and environmental circumstances at that particular time and place. One possible consequence is overexploitation of subsistence resources, to the extent that the land becomes uninhabitable or the population must drop to a much lower density. In other situations, introduction of a new trait may enhance the productivity of subsistence techniques, providing a basis for the support of a higher population concentration and increased cultural complexity.

One of the most interesting illustrations of the relationship between environment and cultural development is provided by the prehistory of the Forests. In both North and South America, relatively advanced configurations arose along the fertile floodplain, where they were sustained initially by prolific wild subsistence resources and later by agriculture. In both regions, the hinterland residents combined wild plant and animal foods with shifting cultivation into a subsistence pattern that was highly reliable as long as population size and density remained relatively low. Until about A.D. 700, parallelism in cultural adaptation is notable; thereafter, however, the two areas began to diverge. In the Eastern Woodlands, the Mississippian culture infiltrated the hinterland, establishing towns with ceremonial structures in the midst of the simpler shifting cultivators. In Amazonia, by contrast, the advanced cultures continued to hug the floodplain until destroyed by European contact. This divergence is not accidental; it reflects the different agricultural potential of these two superficially similar Forest environments.

The North American Forest is a Type 3 environment. Fertile soils of glacial and alluvial origin occur outside the active floodplains, and the Mississippians had achieved sufficient agricultural sophistication to seek them out for cultivation. Although temperate soils are subject to depletion under intensive cropping, the process is slower than in the tropics because high temperatures are restricted to a few summer months and annual rainfall is significantly less. These conditions not only reduce the rate of erosion and nutrient loss, but also enhance the efficacy of restorative measures such as fertilization, crop rotation, and fallowing. Clean clearing with exposure of the bare soil during a large part of the year, and planting of extensive areas with wheat, maize, or some other uniform crop are among intensive techniques of temperate agriculture that have disastrous consequences when applied in the tropics.

Amazonia is an excellent example of a Type 2 environment, with limited agricultural potential. Soils outside the floodplain of the Amazon and a few of its tributaries are infertile as a consequence of continuous exposure to high temperature combined with heavy rainfall. Under the protection of the forest, leaching and erosion are minimized; once the vegetation is removed, however, soluble nutrients are swiftly lost. Since modern technology remains unsuccessful in counteracting these environmental deficiencies, it is not surprising that aboriginal floodplain farmers were unable to transplant their advanced culture to the hinterland. Unfortunately, the superficial resemblance of Amazonia to other forested regions more suitable for intensive cultivation has not only hampered understanding of its role in New World cultural development, but has led to unrealistic expectations about its capacity to sustain the burgeoning population of today's world.

181

The failure of cultures along the Brazilian coast to reach a higher level of complexity has another explanation. Most of this Forest region falls into Type 3; however, it was isolated from potential diffusion sources in the Andean and Desert Areas by a broad expanse of uncultivable terrain. Even after contact was established, the effect was weakened by environmental differences between the donor and recipient areas, which made introduced cultigens and agricultural techniques less productive than they otherwise might have been. The contrast in aboriginal cultural complexity between the Brazilian coastal Forest and the Eastern Woodlands of North America highlights the importance of access to an appropriate source of diffusion for the realization of the potential inherent in a Type 3 environment.

The arid portions of the Pacific Coasts are a pair of Type 3 areas that provide another marked precolumbian contrast. In California, a productive hunting and gathering economy was perpetuated until European contact. In northern Chile, on the other hand, agriculture was adopted shortly after its introduction into the adjacent Desert of northwestern Argentina. Several factors appear to be responsible for this difference in subsistence pattern and associated cultural complexity. One is geographical location. In North America, the Desert abuts the most arid portion of the Pacific Coast, where agriculture without elaborate irrigation measures is unprofitable. Thus, in the zone where influences would have been strongest, they encountered greatest resistance. In South America, by contrast, the mutual frontier extends southward to the Transversal Valleys of central Chile, where conditions resembling those of the adjacent portion of the Desert Area facilitated the exchange of cultural elements. In addition, the north Chilean coast was readily accessible and environmentally similar to southern Peru, whereas coastal California was isolated from highly developed portions of Mesoamerica. Receptivity to diffusion was also affected by the differing subsistence resources of the two Pacific Coastal Areas. In California, the high productivity of wild foods permitted the development of subsistence patterns that were as rewarding as agriculture, if not more so. In Chile, the wild resources were less prolific and agriculture served as a welcome supplement that enhanced subsistence security.

The importance of specialized technology for realization of the agricultural potential of Type 3 environments is further illustrated by the contrast between the aboriginal utilization of the Deserts, Plains, and North American Forests and modern intensive exploitation of these regions. Type 3 areas generally suffer from one or more natural deficiencies that restrict agricultural productivity in the absence of scientific knowledge or technological capacity sufficiently advanced to identify and counteract them. In the Plains, digging sticks and other hand tools were inefficient for removal of the heavy sod, and agriculture was consequently confined mainly to river bottoms before the introduction of the plow, and more recently, mechanical equipment. In the Deserts, water must often be brought from long distances or great depths, both solutions requiring the application of advanced engineering skills. In other situations, sophisticated botanical knowledge may be needed to identify nutrient deficiencies or to design crop rotation schedules that will conserve soil fertility. Under these circumstances, adaptive processes can be expected to favor refinement in the utilization of wild food resources, rather than intensification of dependence on agriculture. Stabilization in level of cultural complexity results.

If the foregoing analysis is provisionally accepted, it raises an important question. What favored the inception of plant domestication in the Nuclear Areas, which have been classified as Type 4 environments? On the basis of evolutionary theory, two general factors seem crucial: (1) wild food resources were not sufficiently dependable to encourage exclusive reliance upon them, and (2) a gradual change in emphasis from wild to domesticated plants could proceed without any lowering of subsistence security during the Transitional Period. It seems probable that tendencies toward incipient agriculture would also be favored by the following kinds of conditions: (1) sufficiently high soil fertility that satisfactory yields could be obtained without fertilization or other restorative measures; (2) natural vegetation sparse enough to make extensive clearing unnecessary; (3) moisture sufficient to permit maturation of the crop, but too low to have significant leaching or erosion potential; (4) moderate temperature minimizing loss from killing frost; (5) wild plant and animal foods in sufficient abundance to serve as a cushion against starvation, but too seasonal, unproductive, limited in nutrients, or in some other respect unsuitable for the establishment of a reliable annual subsistence cycle. These are, in fact, the features that pertain in many parts of Mesoamerica and the Andean Area.

183

Agriculture must have originally been merely a means of fortifying the hunting and gathering subsistence pattern. Everything known about the evolutionary process indicates that natural selection preserves innovations that improve however slightly an existing pattern of adaptation and eliminates those that diminish its effectiveness. The first steps toward food production may consequently have been efforts to increase the abundance of a plant that matured at a time when other resources were scarce. As these measures met with increasing success, emphasis could gradually shift away from some of the less dependable wild foods. Little by little, awareness would develop of ways in which places not naturally suitable for planting could be made productive, and the most obvious of these was probably the addition of water. Where rivers or springs coincide with fertile soils, as they do in parts of Nuclear America, even the most rudimentary forms of irrigation were likely to increase the harvest. As understanding grew, water distribution measures were elaborated and larger amounts of land were brought under cultivation. Alternatively, the moisture provided by seasonal rainfall could be utilized to better advantage by planting in low places, where evaporation was retarded, or by constructing impediments to runoff, beginning with a row of stones, a ditch, or a ridge and developing ultimately into a system of hillside terraces. Once this kind of process was initiated it would accelerate, because human intervention of whatever kind would modify the productivity, density, range, variability, and other characteristics of the plants involved, with consequences that would in turn affect their use. Whatever the sequence of events, the achievement of intensive agriculture in Mesoamerica and the Andean Area required not only centuries but millennia. The process must have been increasingly productive both qualitatively and quantitatively, however, or it would have been truncated at some lower level, as it was elsewhere in the Americas.

A number of authorities have suggested that the crucial aspect of the Nuclear Areas was the large amount of uncultivatable land, and that civilization arose in response to population pressure on finite agricultural resources. Conversely, the failure of high culture to develop in the Amazon basin has been attributed to the unlimited availability of agricultural land, which encouraged dispersal of the population rather than intensification of local subsistence exploitation (e.g. Carneiro,

184

1961). This hypothesis incorporates two assumptions that are open to question: (1) that population increase precedes rather than follows expansion in subsistence productivity, and (2) that the Amazon basin was underpopulated at the time of European contact. A considerable amount of evidence from animal population studies indicates that density rises when the food supply increases and falls when it declines, although the two cycles are seldom in perfect coordination because the reproductive process of higher animals is too slow to respond immediately to changes in subsistence level. If the population outruns the food supply, possible consequences include elimination of the excess by death or emigration, intensification of subsistence exploitation with resultant depletion of the resources (which merely postpones the population decline), or enlargement of the food supply by measures that are not environmentally destructive. Which alternative is implemented by man depends both on the nature of the cultural configuration and on the agricultural potential of the environment it occupies. If increased productivity is precluded, as it is in a Type 2 environment, population decline will occur immediately or following a period of overexploitation and consequent damage to the habitat. If the agricultural potential has not been realized, the same result may follow unless improved methods of soil conservation or water distribution are developed, or a higher yielding cultigen is produced. If the technology is adequate and the environment is receptive, population density can continue to increase. It is important to recognize that all these aspects are operating simultaneously, with the result that an effort to distinguish cause from effect is likely to obscure rather than clarify the evolutionary process.

With the possible exception of the Andean Area, the evidence suggests that an equilibrium had been reached in precolumbian America between population density and the carrying capacity of the various kinds of environments, given the subsistence technology that was available. Although it has sometimes been asserted that the Eastern Woodlands and the Amazonian lowlands were underpopulated, the number and variety of cultural mechanisms inhibiting increases in density that existed among aboriginal groups in both regions argue forcefully against such an interpretation. In other cases, notably the Southwestern United States, an equilibrium adaptation was apparently upset in late prehistoric times by climatic changes, with resultant reduction in community size and abandonment of formerly productive localities. Occasionally overexploitation led to environmental degradation and population decline, a process that has been invoked to explain the abandonment of Tula (Cook, 1949) and the downfall of Classic Maya civilization.

Cultural ecologists are sometimes accused of emphasizing the environment, and specifically technology, at the expense of social and religious factors in explaining cultural evolution. In some instances, the accusation is true, but the emphasis is justifiable since there is an upper limit to the extent to which the food supply can be increased and this places a ceiling on cultural development. There are few if any "environmentalists," however, who view cultural adaptation from so narrow a perspective. Perhaps better than other kinds of anthropologists, they appreciate the complexity of the adaptive process and the intricate interlacing of customs, beliefs, techniques, and other kinds of behavior with each other and with the environment. Because of the complexity of this interrelationship, it is seldom possible to distinguish cause from effect. A culture is a balanced system, in which all parts preserve enough flexibility to permit their constant accommodation to alterations of cultural or environmental derivation. To assert that social organization, population pressure, or some other single factor was the cause of cultural advance is unrealistic. It is more fruitful to compare the histories of cultures possessing different types of social integration and settlement pattern, to see whether one form was more successful than another, and if so, to discover if possible where the superiority lay. As with biological genera and families, some of the cultural extinctions probably resulted from natural disasters, in which case they tell us only that the adaptive process was too slow for accommodation to rapid alterations in the environment. Such instances were probably rare, however, and the thousands of cultures that have existed along with the hundreds that remain to some degree intact offer many opportunities to gather significant information for the clarification of the relationship between environment and culture.

Viewing cultural development in prehistoric America in ecological perspective reveals parallels in adaptation to environmentally similar but geographically isolated portions of the hemisphere that are far too numerous and specific to be the product of chance. To the extent that they are not accidental, they must be determined. This is not

186

equivalent to asserting that they were preordained. Each region was subjected to natural and historical accidents that affected the result. In view of the complexity of the culture-environment relationship, however, the similarities in content and in general cultural history in each pair of environmentally comparable regions are remarkable. A better understanding of their origin will not only help to explain what happened in the past, but will clarify the nature and intensity of environmental constraints on present and future cultural development, not only in the Americas but on the planet as a whole.

Selected References

Most of the works in the "General" section contain extensive bibliographies and several (especially Jennings 1968 and Willey 1966, 1971) are well illustrated. They should be consulted in addition to the references provided for each topic.

GENERAL

Jennings, Jesse D.
  1968   *Prehistory of North America*. New York, McGraw-Hill.
Jennings, Jesse D., Editor
  1978   *Ancient native* **Americans. San Francisco, W. H. Freeman and Co.**
Meggers, Betty J. and Clifford Evans, Editors
  1963   *Aboriginal cultural development in Latin America: an interpretative review*. Washington, Smithsonian Institution.
Sanders, William T. and Joseph Marino
  1970   *New World prehistory*. Englewood Cliffs, Prentice-Hall.
Steward, Julian H., Editor
  1946–1959   *Handbook of South American Indians*. Bureau of American Ethnology Bul. 143, Vols. 1–7. Washington, Smithsonian Institution.
Wauchope, Robert, Editor
  1964–1976   *Handbook of Middle American Indians*. Austin, Univ. Texas Press.

Willey, Gordon R.

1966 *An introduction to American archaeology; North and Middle America.* New York, Prentice-Hall.

1971 *An introduction to American archaeology; South America.* New York, Prentice-Hall.

PRE-PROJECTILE POINT, PALEO-INDIAN
AND TRANSITIONAL PERIODS

Aveleyra Arroyo de Anda, Luis

1964 "The primitive hunters." *Handbook of Middle American Indians*, Robert Wauchope, Ed., 1:384–412. Austin, Univ. of Texas Press.

Bird, Junius B.

1969 "A comparison of south Chilean and Ecuadorian 'fishtail' projectile points." *The Kroeber Anthropological Society Papers* 40:52–71. Berkeley.

Bryan, Alan L., Editor

1978 *Early man in America from a circum-pacific perspective.* Occasional Papers 1, Department of Anthropology, Univ. of Alberta, Edmonton.

Byers, Douglas S.

1957 "The Bering Bridge—some speculations." *Ethnos* 1–2:20–26. Stockholm.

Dragoo, Don W.

1968 "Early lithic cultures of the New World." *Proceedings of the 8th International Congress of Anthropological and Ethnological Sciences* 3:175–176. Tokyo.

Frison, George C.

1978 *Prehistoric hunters of the high plains.* New York, Academic Press.

Hester, James J.

1966 "Origins of the Clovis culture." *XXXVI Congreso Internacional de Americanistas, Actas y Memorias* 1:129–142. Sevilla.

Krieger, Alex D.

1964 "Early man in the New World." *Prehistoric man in the New World*, Jesse D. Jennings and Edward Norbeck, Eds., pp. 23–81. Chicago, Univ. of Chicago Press.

Lanning, Edward P. and E. A. Hammel

1961 "Early lithic industries of western South America." *American Antiquity* 27:139–154.

Lynch, Thomas F. and Kenneth A. R. Kennedy
   1970   "Early human cultural and skeletal remains from Guitarrero Cave, northern Peru." *Science* 169:1307–9.
Müller-Beck, Hansjürgen
   1966   "Paleohunters in America; origins and diffusion." *Science* 152:1191–1210.
Schobinger, Juan
   1969   *Prehistoria de Suramérica.* Barcelona, Editorial Labor.
Wendorf, Fred
   1966   "Early man in the New World; problems of migration." *The American Naturalist* 100:253–270.

ORIGIN OF AGRICULTURE

Mangelsdorf, Paul C., Richard S. MacNeish and Gordon R. Willey
   1964   "Origins of agriculture in Middle America." *Handbook of Middle American Indians,* Robert Wauchope, Ed., 1:427–445. Austin, Univ. of Texas Press.
MacNeish, Richard S., Antoinette Nelken-Terner and Angel García Cook
   1970   *Second annual report of the Ayacucho archaeological-botanical project.* Andover, Phillips Academy.
Patterson, Thomas C. and M. Edward Moseley
   1968   "Late preceramic and early ceramic cultures of the central coast of Peru." *Nawpa Pacha* 6:115–133.

INTRODUCTION AND DIFFUSION OF POTTERY

Ford, James A.
   1969   *A comparison of Formative cultures in the Americas; diffusion or the psychic unity of man?* Smithsonian Contributions to Anthropology 11. Washington.
Kehoe, Alice B.
   1962   "A hypothesis on the origin of northeastern American pottery." *Southwestern Journal of Anthropology* 18:20–29.
Meggers, Betty J., Clifford Evans and Emilio Estrada
   1965   *Early Formative period of coastal Ecuador; the Valdivia and Machalilla phases.* Smithsonian Contributions to Anthropology 1. Washington.

Bernal, Ignacio
1969   *The Olmec world.* Berkeley, Univ. of California Press.
Cieza de León, Pedro de
1959   *The Incas of Pedro de Cieza de León.* Norman, Univ. of Oklahoma Press.
Coe, Michael D.
1966   *The Maya.* New York, Praeger.
Diaz del Castillo, Bernal
1927   *The true history of the conquest of Mexico.* New York, Robert M. McBride.
Evans, Clifford and Betty J. Meggers
1966   "Mesoamerica and Ecuador." *Handbook of Middle American Indians,* Robert Wauchope, Ed., 4:243–264. Austin, Univ. of Texas Press.
Lumbreras, Luis G.
1974   *Peoples and cultures of ancient Peru.* Washington, Smithsonian Institution Press.
MacNeish, Richard S.
1967–   *The prehistory of the Tehuacán valley.* Austin, Univ. of Texas Press.
Meggers, Betty J.
1966   *Ecuador.* New York, Praeger.
Reichel-Dolmatoff, Gerardo
1965   *Colombia.* New York, Praeger.
Rouse, Irving
1964   "Prehistory of the West Indies." *Science* 144:499–513.
Rouse, Irving and José M. Cruxent
1963   **Venezuelan archeology. New Haven, Yale Univ. Press.**
Sámanos, Juan de
1844   "Relación de los primeros descubrimientos de Francisco Pizarro y Diego de Almagro." *Colección de documentos inéditos para la historia de España* 5:193–201. Madrid.
Sanders, William T. and Barbara J. Price
1968   *Mesoamerica; the evolution of a civilization.* New York, Random House.
Smith, Bradley
1962   *Columbus in the New World.* New York, Doubleday.

THE FORESTS

Brochado, José Proenza and Others
1970 "Brazilian archaeology in 1968." *American Antiquity* 35:1–23.
Caldwell, Joseph R.
1958 *Trend and tradition in the prehistory of the eastern United States.* American Anthropological Association Memoir 88.
Dragoo, Don W.
1963 *Mounds for the dead; an analysis of the Adena culture.* Annals of the Carnegie Museum 37. Pittsburgh.
Evans, Clifford and Betty J. Meggers
1968 **Archeological investigations on the Rio Nap, eastern Ecuador. Smithsonian Contributions to Anthropology 6. Washington.**
Griffin, James B.
1967 "Eastern North American archaeology, a summary." *Science* 156:175–191.

THE DESERTS

Gonzalez, Alberto Rex
1961 "The La Aguada culture of northwestern Argentina." *Essays in pre-Columbian art and archaeology,* S. K. Lothrop and Others, pp. 389–420. Cambridge, Harvard Univ. Press.
Kelley, J. Charles
1966 "Mesoamerica and the Southwestern United States." *Handbook of Middle American Indians,* Robert Wauchope, Ed., 4:95–110. Austin, Univ. of Texas Press.
Martin, Paul S. and John B. Rinaldo
1951 "The Southwestern co-tradition." *Southwestern Journal of Anthropology* 7:215–229.
Palevecino, Enrique
1948 "Areas y capas culturales en el territorio argentino." *Anales de la Sociedad Argentina de Estudios Geográficos* 8:447–523. Buenos Aires.

THE PLAINS

Cooper, John M.
1946 "The Patagonian and Pampean hunters." *Handbook of South*

American Indians, Julian H. Steward, Ed., 1:127–168. Washington, Smithsonian Institution.

Oliver, Symmes C.
  1968 "Ecology and cultural continuity as contributing factors in the social organization of the Plains Indians." *Man in adaptation; the cultural present,* Yehudi A. Cohen, Ed., pp. 244–262. Chicago, Aldine.

Wedel, Waldo R.
  1961 *Prehistoric man on the Great Plains.* Norman, Univ. of Oklahoma Press.

Willey, Gordon R.
  1946 "The archeology of the Greater Pampa." *Handbook of South American Indians,* Julian H. Steward, Ed., 1:25–46. Washington, Smithsonian Institution.

Winship, George Parker
  1896 "The Coronado expedition, 1540–1542." *Bureau of American Ethnology, 14th Annual Report,* Part 1:329–613. Washington, Smithsonian Institution.

THE PACIFIC COASTS

Darwin, Charles
  1871 *Journal of researches into the natural history and geology of the countries visited during the voyage of H.M.S. Beagle round the world.* New York, D. Appleton.

Heizer, Robert F.
  1964 "The western coast of North America." *Prehistoric man in the New World,* Jesse D. Jennings and Edward Norbeck, Eds., pp. 117–148. Chicago, Univ. of Chicago Press.

Núñez Atencio, Lautaro
  1969 "Panorama arqueológico del norte de Chile." *Mesa redonda de ciencias prehistóricas y antropológicas* 2:197–217. Lima, Pontificia Universidad Católica del Perú.

THE MARGINALS

Cooper, John M.
  1941 *Temporal sequence and the Marginal cultures.* Washington, Catholic Univ. of America.

Jennings, Jesse D.
  1957   *Danger Cave.* University of Utah Anthropological Papers 27. Salt
        Lake City.
Lowie, Robert H.
  1946   "Eastern Brazil; an introduction." *Handbook of South American
        Indians,* Julian H. Steward, Ed., 1:381–397. Washington, Smith-
        sonian Institution.
Métraux, Alfred
  1939   "Myths and tales of the Matako Indians." *Ethnologiska Studier*
        9:1–127. Göteborg.
Nordenskiold, Erland
  1931   *Origin of the Indian civilizations in South America.* Comparative
        Ethnographic Studies 9. Göteborg.
Steward, Julian H.
  1938   *Basin-plateau aboriginal sociopolitical groups.* Bureau of American
        Ethnology Bul. 120. Washington, Smithsonian Institution.

THE ARCTIC

Collins, Henry B.
  1964   "The arctic and subarctic." *Prehistoric man in the New World,*
        Jesse D. Jennings and Edward Norbeck, Eds., pp. 85–114. Chicago,
        Univ. of Chicago Press.
MacNeish, Richard S.
  1964   "Investigations in southwest Yukon; archaeological excavation, com-
        parisons and speculations." *Papers of the Peabody Foundation for
        Archaeology* 6, part 2. Andover.

PROBLEMS AND SPECULATIONS

Adams, Robert McC.
  1966   *The evolution of urban society.* Chicago, Aldine.
Ashe, Geoffrey and Others
  1971   *The quest for America.* New York, Praeger.
Carneiro, Robert L.
  1961   "Slash-and-burn cultivation among the Kuikuru and its implications
        for cultural development in the Amazon Basin." *The evolution of
        horticultural systems in native South America; causes and conse-*

quences, Johannes Wilbert, Ed., pp. 47–67. Caracas, Sociedad de Ciencias Naturales La Salle.

Cook, Sherburne F.
1949 *The historical demography and ecology of the Teotlalpan.* Ibero-Americana 33. Berkeley and Los Angeles, Univ. of California Press.

Harner, Michael J.
1970 "Population pressure and the social evolution of agriculturalists." *Southwestern Journal of Anthropology* 26:67–86.

Jett, Stephen C.
1978 **"Pre-columbian transoceanic contacts."** *Ancient native Americans,* **Jesse D. Jennings, Ed., pp. 593-650. San Francisco, W. H. Freeman and Co.**

Meggers, Betty J.
1954 "Environmental limitation on the development of culture." *American Anthropologist* 56:801–824.
1964 "North and South American cultural connections and convergences." *Prehistoric man in the New World,* Jesse D. Jennings and Edward Norbeck, Eds., pp. 511–526. Chicago, Univ. of Chicago Press.

Riley, Carroll L. and Others
1971 *Man across the sea; problems of pre-Columbian contacts.* Austin, Univ. of Texas Press.

Watson, Adam, Editor
1970 *Animal populations in relation to their food resources.* Oxford and Edinburgh, Blackwell Scientific Publications.

The illustrations have been compiled from a variety of published and unpublished sources, and the cooperation of the many individuals and institutions involved is formally and gratefully acknowledged. Differences in content, character, and origin require division of accreditation into several categories. Where only author and date are provided, the complete citation can be found in the "Selected References." Except where otherwise specified, line drawings are by George Robert Lewis.

FIGURES REDRAWN FROM PUBLICATIONS

Fig. 2b, after Bormida, Marcelo, *Arqueología de la costa norpatagónica*, Univ. de Madrid, 1964; 2c–2e, after Sellards, E. H., "Some early stone artifact developments in North America," *Southwestern Journal of Anthropology* 16:160–173, 1960.

Fig. 3, after Lumbreras, 1969.

Figs. 5a, 5c–5e, after Jennings, 1968; 5b after Sellards, E. H., *Early man in America*, Austin, Univ. of Texas Press, 1952; 5f–5h, after Aveleyra Arroyo de Anda, Luis, *Los cazadores primitivos en Mesoamérica*, México, Univ. Nac. Autónoma de México, 1967; 5i–5j, after Bird, Junius, "A comparison of south Chilean and Ecuadorian 'fishtail' projective points," *The Kroeber Anthropological Society Papers* 40, 1969.

Fig. 6a–6c, after Jennings, 1968; 6d, after Sellards, 1952; 6e–6f, after Willey, 1966; 6g–6h, after Schobinger, 1969.

Fig. 9a–9j, after Lewis, Thomas M. N. and Madeline K. Lewis, *Eva, an archaic site*, Knoxville, Univ. of Tenn. Press, 1961; 9k–9o, after Ritchie, William A., *The archaeology of New York state*, Garden City, Natural History Press, 1969; 9p, after Jennings, 1968.

Fig. 10, after MacNeish, Richard S., *Second annual report of the Tehuacán Archaeological-Botanical Project*, Andover, Phillips Academy, 1962.

Figs. 12a–12c, after Gajardo Tobar, Roberto, "Investigaciones arqueológicas en la desembocadura del río Choapa," *Anales de Arqueología* 17–18, Mendoza, 1962–63; 12d–12f, after Eberhart, H., "The cogged stones of southern California," *American Antiquity* 26: 361–369, 1961.

Fig. 19a, after Borhegyi, Stephen F., *A study of three-pronged incense burners from Guatemala and adjacent areas*, Washington, Carnegie Institution, 1951.

Fig. 20a, after Coe, Michael D., *The jaguar's children: pre-classic central Mexico*, New York, Museum of Primitive Art, 1965.

Fig. 37, after Coe, 1966.

Fig. 45, after Lumbreras, Luis G., *Los templos de Chavín*, Lima, Corporación Peruana del Santa, 1970.

Fig. 48, after photograph by Ramiro Matos Mendieta.

Fig. 49, after Lothrop, Samuel K., *Treasures of ancient America*, Cleveland, World Publishing Co.

Fig. 53, after Steward, J. H., Ed., *Handbook of South American Indians*, Vol 2, Smithsonian Institution, 1946.

Figs. 57a, 57c, after Zevallos Menéndez, Carlos, "Tecnología metalúrgica arqueológica; elaboración del alambre," *Cuadernos de Historia y Arqueología* 6:5–11, Guayaquil, Casa de la Cultura Ecuatoriana, 1958; 57b, after Huerta Rendón, F., "El Museo de Oro de la Casa de la Cultura del Guayas," *Vistazo* 81:14–17, Guayaquil, 1964.

Fig. 65, after Reichel-Dolmatoff, 1965.

Figs. 67 and 68, after Perez de Barradas, José, *Orfebrería prehispánica de Colombia; estilos Tolima y Muisca*, Madrid, Banco de la República (Bogotá), 1958.

Fig. 71, after Shetrone, Henry C., *The mound-builders*, New York, D. Appleton, 1930.

Fig. 72, after Binford, S. R., and L. R. Binford, *New perspectives in archeology*, Chicago, Aldine, 1968.

Fig. 80, after Meggers, Betty J., *Amazonia*, Chicago and New York, Aldine•Atherton, 1971.

Fig. 82, culture areas after Jennings, 1968.

Fig. 83, after Covarrubias, Miguel, *The eagle, the jaguar and the serpent*, New York, Knopf, 1954; Fewkes, J. W., "Designs on prehistoric Hopi pottery," *Bureau of American Ethnology, 33rd Annual Report*, Washington, Smithsonian Institution, 1919; Martin, Paul S. and Elizabeth S. Willis, *Anasazi painted pottery in the Field Museum of Natural History*, Chicago, Field Museum, 1940; Smith, Watson, *Painted ceramics of the Western Mount at Awatovi*, Cambridge, Harvard University, 1971.

Fig. 84b, after Ibarra Grasso, Dick Edgar, *Argentina indígena*, Buenos Aires, Tipográfica Editora Argentina, 1967.

Fig. 86, after Covarrubias, 1954.

Fig. 88, after Ibarra Grasso, 1967.

Fig. 89, after Serrano, Antonio, *Consideraciones sobre el arte y la cronología en la región diaguita*, Rosario, Univ. Nac. del Litoral, 1953.

Fig. 90, after Serrano, 1953 and Serrano, Antonio, *El arte decorativo de los Diaguitas*, Córdoba, Univ. Nac. de Córdoba, 1943.

Fig. 92, after Smith, C. S. and A. E. Johnson, *The Two Teeth site*, Pubs. in Salvage Archeology 8, Smithsonian Institution, 1968.

Fig. 93, after Willey 1966; drawing by Marcia Bakry.

Fig. 94, after *Bureau of American Ethnology, 10th Annual Report*, Washington, Smithsonian Institution, 1893.

Fig. 97, after Steward, 1938.

Fig. 98, after Collins, Henry B., *Archeology of St. Lawrence Island, Alaska*, Smithsonian Misc. Collections, Washington, 1937.

Fig. 100, after Boas, Franz, *The central Eskimo*, Washington, Smithsonian Institution, 1888.

FIGURES DRAWN FROM SPECIMENS OR PHOTOGRAPHS

Figs. 2a, 4, 11, National Museum of Natural History, Smithsonian Institution.

Fig. 19b, Museo Arqueológico del Banco Central, Quito.

Fig. 20b, Museo Arqueológico "Víctor Emilio Estrada", Guayaquil.

Fig. 25, Dumbarton Oaks Collection, Washington.

Fig. 34, University Museum, Philadelphia.

Fig. 64, Mario Sanoja.

Fig. 75, Museum of the American Indian, Heye Foundation, New York.

Fig. 84a, Cambridge University Museum of Archeology and Ethnology, England.

DRAWINGS REPRODUCED FROM PUBLICATIONS

Fig. 8, Wedel, Waldo R., Wilfred M. Husted and John H. Moss, "Mummy Cave: prehistoric record from Rocky Mountains of Wyoming," *Science* 160:184–186, 1968.

Fig. 17, Ford, 1969.

Fig. 22, Drucker, Philip, Robert F. Heiser and R. J. Squier, *Excavations at La Venta, Tabasco, 1955*, Washington, Smithsonian Institution, 1959.

Fig. 27, Linné, S., *Mexican highland cultures, archaeological researches at Teotihuacán, Calpulalpán and Chalchicomula in 1934-5*, Stockholm, Ethnographical Museum of Sweden, 1942.

Figs. 33, 38, Spinden, Herbert J., *Maya art and civilization*, Indian Hills, Colo., The Falcon's Wing Press, 1957.

Fig. 46, Lumbreras, Luis G., *Los templos de Chavín*, Lima, Corporación Peruana del Santa, 1970.

Fig. 55, Willey, Gordon R., *Prehistoric settlement patterns in the Virú Valley, Perú*, Washington, Smithsonian Instiution, 1953.

Fig. 60, Steward, J. H., Ed., *Handbook of South American Indians*, Vol. 2, Washington, Smithsonian Institution, 1946.

Fig. 70, Ford, James A. and Clarence H. Webb, *Poverty Point, a late archaic site in Louisiana*, New York, American Museum of Natural History, 1956.

Figs. 74, 77, De Bry, Theodore, *Grands et petits voyages*, 1591.

Fig. 81, Steward, J. H., Ed., *Handbook of South American Indians*, Vol. 3, Washington, Smithsonian Institution, 1948.

Fig. 99, Boas, 1888.

PHOTOGRAPHS AND/OR PERMISSION FOR THEIR PUBLICATION

Figs. 14–15, 19, 26, 28–32, 40–41, 52, 58–59, 62, 78–79, 85, Clifford Evans.

Fig. 23, Irmgard Groth-Kimball.

Figs. 24, 50, 66, 76, National Museum of Natural History, Smithsonian Institution.

Fig. 35, Carnegie Institution of Washington.

Figs. 39, 43, Museo Nacional de Antropología, México.

Fig. 42, Bodleian Library, Oxford.

Fig. 47, Ethel Ford.

Fig. 51, The Cleveland Museum of Art, the Norweb Collection.

Figs. 54, 56, Servicio Aerofotográfico Nacional, Peru.

Fig. 61, Aerial Explorations Inc., 1931.

Fig. 73, Peabody Museum of Archaeology and Ethnology, Harvard University.

Figs. 91, 96, National Anthropological Archives, Smithsonian Institution.

Fig. 95, Junius Bird, 1935, American Museum of Natural History.

IDENTIFICATION OF DECORATIVE MOTIFS

Cover, Lintel of the Jaguars, Chavín de Huántar, Peru; Title page, Bahia pottery figurine, coastal Ecuador; Page viii, Flat pottery stamp, Tlatilco, Mexico; Page 6, Pictographs from Ohio (footprints) and Chile (running figures); Page 44, Cylindrical pottery stamp, Valley of Mexico; Page 110, Painted pottery design, Rio Napo, eastern Ecuador; Page 152, Yurok-Karok basketry design, northwestern California; Page 172, Painted pottery designs, Coclé culture, Panama.

Index

198